W9-AIA-759

Soul Tending

MANUFACTURED IN THE UNITED STATES OF AMERICA

07 08 09 10 11 12 13 14 15 16 — 10 9 8 7 6 5 4 3 2

ISBN: 9780687642908

Cover Design: Keely Moore

Contents

3

Contributors 143

4

Foreword

This will completely reveal my inner-nerdiness, but I wish John Wesley were alive today so that he could be my best friend. That guy was intense about following Jesus. He wouldn't settle for half-hearted anything, especially not a lukewarm commitment to Christ. I've always wanted to be near Wesley in the hopes that his passion and zeal would spill over onto me. Reading his understanding and explanation of the "means of grace"—practices that put us in a place where we are transformed by God's grace—awakened my heart and opened my eyes to see and know God like I never had before.

Wesley was all about practicing his faith. With him you were either moving forward in faith or going backward. And the way to move forward or go deeper in faith was to practice it. Christians have all sorts of names for the ways we practice our faith: means of grace, spiritual disciplines, holy ordinances, practices of faith, holy habits. These are the ways that we come to know God more fully and through which we participate in God's action in the world. Wesley explained means of grace as works of piety and works of mercy. The balanced spiritual life attended both to piety—prayer, study, worship—and mercy— giving to the poor, visiting the sick, serving others. A Christian who practices works of piety has a deeper well of God's grace and love to share with others through works of mercy.

In college I delved into Wesley's sermons and other classic theological works, and I was convinced that in all my years of faith, I had never really known God. Turns out that spiritual discipline doesn't mean sitting still in church and "just saying no." I've discovered instead that spiritual discipline requires me to make space in my heart and life for time with God: time when I can know God, sense God's presence, and experience what it is like to be known by God. That doesn't happen just by staying busy with "church stuff."

SOUL TENDING helps you be intentional about "tending" to your relationship with God and opening your heart to the activity of God in your life. God is working and doing things all around you. The spiritual practices described in this book allow you to participate with God—they make you more aware of the grace of God that is readily available to you.

Richard Foster, author of *Celebration of Discipline*, explains that grace is not a form of sin-management. This important insight was a revelation to me because I had always believed that grace was nothing more than "that thing that fixes sin." But Foster mentions in his writing and speaking that grace is something much bigger: It

is the ongoing work of God in and through us. By grace we are free from sin, but because of grace we are free for a life with God. Through spiritual practices, we become aware of this grace, claim the freedom that God offers us, and participate in God's ongoing work of salvation.

A few years ago I was on a mission to help young people know God through spiritual practice. So I gathered a group of youth pastors and friends who shared my passion. We dreamed about teenagers and young adults covenanting together to practice the means of grace and see what God would do in their lives. Out of that came the small group resource, *Soul Tending: Life-Forming Practices for Older Youth and Young Adults.*

In the five years since it has been in publication, I have heard story after story of youth groups devoting themselves to prayer and re-imagining their understanding of what it means to follow Jesus. I've heard of groups of college students choosing a faith practice for weeks at a time and holding one another accountable for sticking with it. The book itself didn't change any lives, but when people look to the ancient practices of faith and open that door to God's grace, a transformation takes place.

This edition of SOUL TENDING is meant for personal use and is the kind of book you'll want to keep next to your bed or in your backpack or purse so that you can use it as a reference or tool to find new ways of opening your heart to God. It's the kind of book that will be a friend, guide, and companion on your faith journey. Pull it out when you want to discover new ways to meet with God or attend to what God is doing in your life. Devote yourself to this life of spiritual practice—of discipline—and you'll find that Christ is being formed in you.

One last warning from John Wesley: "Remember also, to use all means, as means; as ordained, not for their own sake, but in order to the renewal of your soul in righteousness and true holiness. If, therefore, they actually tend to this, well; but if not, they are dung and dross."[1] This is his intense way (because he has no other way) of saying that the practices themselves are not what change us. God changes us. The practices help us train our minds and hearts to see what God is already doing in our lives and join in.

My prayer for you is that, as you take on a life of spiritual practice, Christ would be formed in you and God's grace would abound in your life. Grace and peace and blessings to you along the way!

—*Jennifer A. Youngman*

Jennifer A. Youngman has worked with youth for over a decade. She is editor of the ABINGDON YOUTH WORSHIP FEAST resource line and developed SOUL TENDING: LIFE-FORMING PRACTICES FOR YOUTH AND YOUNG ADULTS. She lives outside Nashville with her husband Mark and children Gracie and Myles.

[1] From John Wesley's "Sermon 16: Means of Grace"

Introduction:
A Spiritual
Formation Journey

By Drew Dyson

The Fast Track

Since my early years in high school, I had been on a spiritual "fast track." I preached my first sermon at the age of fifteen. I served on several committees in my local church. In my junior and senior years, I was president of the church youth group. After a brief period of vocational struggle, I went to college where I majored in youth ministry. I began my first full-time youth ministry job at the age of twenty. Then at twenty-two, I moved to a larger church and began seminary. My life, my spiritual journey, and my career were all on "overdrive." Then came the wall.

The Wall

Trying to keep pace on this fast track left me completely exhausted and on the verge of burnout. For years I had been living out my faith in a subconscious attempt to achieve "super-Christian" status. For me, it was an effort to earn the love and acceptance of God when I was struggling to love myself. I believed that trying harder, doing more, learning more, and teaching more would eventually get me the love I craved and fill my inner longing. I would finally be the person that God wanted me to be.

9

I professed just the opposite. I told others of a loving God in Jesus Christ who accepts us where we are. Yet I lived as if I were a kindergartner earning stickers for significant milestones or a football player earning decals for great plays. I had gold stars from great insights in Sunday School, grades that I received, and people whom I had helped. I was trying to become a spiritual superstar to earn God's love.

The warning signs had been flashing for months. My prayer life had become virtually non-existent. The only time I opened my Bible was to prepare for a lesson or a sermon. My time and energy at work were spent on creating activities and programs at church rather than creating opportunities for young people to enter into a life-transforming relationship with the risen Christ. By all accounts, I was well on my way to reaching superstar status. People encouraged me to "reach for the stars" and congratulated me each time I climbed another rung on the spiritual ladder. Pretty soon, my ego outweighed my faith, but I was the only one who knew that. The outward signs of my faith remained shiny and strong, but inside, I'd hit the wall.

The Question

The question came out of nowhere and pierced the deafening silence of my spiritual life: "How is it with your soul?" she asked. Julie was a high school junior who consistently attended our youth group events and activities. She was quiet, slightly withdrawn, and very awkward around other people. She and I never seemed to connect—until that night.

She pressed on, "You always ask us that question. I just wasn't sure if anyone ever asked you, so I thought

I would. I just wanted you to know that I care." Stumbling, I answered her question. But by looking into her eyes, I knew I

wasn't fooling her. Soon, everyone went home. I went to my car and started the engine. When the parking lot was empty, the tears came easily. I knew that my spiritual life had been dry for months, but now so did someone else.

A Turning Point

In an effort to jump start my spiritual life, I attended a retreat designed to help me develop spiritual practices. At the outset, I was looking for a quick fix to an enduring problem. I wanted to be able to go home and give Julie an answer to her question. But somewhere, in the stillness of a morning walk on a mountain path, God showed up.

That morning I read John 1:35-37 where Jesus calls his first disciples. John the Baptist is sitting by the side of the road with a couple of his disciples when Jesus passes by. John sees Jesus coming and points him out to his disciples, "Look, the Lamb of God!" The disciples turn and immediately follow Jesus.

On that mountain path, I realized that I was overwhelmed by the exhaustion of "pointing" to Jesus. The problem was, unlike John, I would not have been able to recognize Jesus if he passed by. I had gotten so busy trying to point Jesus out to others that I became disconnected from the Jesus who longed to be in relationship with me. I longed to know Christ, yet the work of my life was to keep up my outward appearances for others while trying to earn God's love.

That weekend was a turning point in my spiritual journey. I realized that in order to be effective in the ministry to which I had been called, I needed to be in an authentic relationship with Jesus Christ. For me, renewing my relationship with Jesus began with accepting God's grace and realizing that God loved me for who I was, not for what I did. My relationship with Christ was freed from the burden of an achievement-oriented faith, and I was able to see myself through Jesus' eyes: a beloved child of God. I realized I needed to "return to my first love" and recapture the passion for my faith that I once held dear.

I needed to fall in love with Christ again and connect to him through spiritual practices and an authentic pursuit of a holy life. I also realized that this change would not be a quick fix. It needed to be a long-term transformation in the way I viewed my spiritual life. My soul was burning out and could not be kept ablaze with anything but the light of Christ.

My deep longing could only be filled by coming into the presence of the Almighty and drinking from the well of life. I needed to "sit at the feet" of the saints—some young and some old—to learn practices of the Christian faith that could help me connect with God. I needed to devote myself to a lifelong journey of spiritual formation.

The Practices

When I was attempting to learn to play the guitar, I bought three different books on the skill for "dummies" and "beginners." I got a great guitar and all of the appropriate equipment and accessories. I practiced the exercises hundreds of times, trying to master the chords and progressions. But after a few months, my family was begging me to give it up—so I did.

After hearing my story, a young friend of mine said that my mistake was that I never actually played, I just practiced. What I should have done, according to this wise, young friend, was turned on the radio or sat with an experienced guitarist and just played along until eventually the sounds blended as one. What he meant was that we cannot do things in isolation, expecting them to miraculously become woven into the fabric and context of our lives. You learn the alphabet letter by letter. While memorizing the alphabet is a good skill to possess, it won't get you very far unless you put the letters together as you read and write.

The same holds true for the Christian faith. Like chords and letters, spiritual practices help us learn how to live a life of faith. But they are more than a tool. They are also the means by which we actually live a life of faith. Christian practices help bring our lives and the life of Christ into a beautiful harmony.

Just as you can't play an instrument or learn to read without practice, you can't live a life of faith without doing the spiritual practices. But if you do the spiritual practices outside the context of a life of faith, you engage in empty rituals.

The Means of Grace

God, through Jesus Christ, has offered to each of us an amazing gift of love that we can never earn and we do not deserve. We call this grace—the free gift of God's love poured out in Jesus Christ. Christian practices are a way or means of receiving that grace into our lives.

Another way to look at this is that the Christian practices put us in the way of grace. They do not help us earn God's grace, which would be an impossible task because grace is free. Rather, the practices of soul tending put us in a place to be transformed by that gift of grace. God uses these means of grace to strengthen God's children and the church for the task of living faithfully as disciples. Christian practices mark us as Christ's disciples and make us into faithful followers formed in the image and likeness of Christ.

This book will teach you about these means of grace, but more importantly, it will guide you in living out these holy habits through which God freely pours out grace upon grace. My prayer is that you will draw near to Jesus, and that, by engaging in the practices described in this book, will advance along a journey that leads to Christ's "being formed in you."

Meditation

The Gift of Meditation

When we think of meditation, sometimes we picture a monk or holy person chanting and sitting in a trance with crossed legs, surrounded by candles and incense. The practice is often associated with Buddhism; but meditation is also a meaningful spiritual discipline that helps us grow as Christian disciples. Meditation is a form of prayer that often involves contemplation, pondering, and thoughtful reflection. When we meditate, we clear our minds and let God do the talking. Meditation is a gift from God that brings us closer to God, our Creator, Redeemer, and Sustainer.

What Is Meditation?

Meditation involves using a particular image or biblical verse to focus our hearts and minds on the presence of God in our midst. Through meditation, we surrender ourselves to God until God's words become our words.

Psalm 119:15-16 says, "I will meditate on your precepts, and fix my eyes on your ways. I will delight in your statutes; I will not forget your word." The people of Israel understood the importance of taking the time to listen to the Word of God through the reading and hearing of the Law or Torah. Many current-day Christians participate in "guided meditations," where a story or a biblical passage is read by a group leader who invites participants to focus on a particular aspect of their faith. In addition to focusing on God mentally, meditation involves a physical stillness and silence to allow, what Thomas Merton—a twentieth-century monk, author, and theologian called—"the echo of God" to resonate through us.

15

How Do We Practice Meditation?

Meditation is not confined to chunks of time we take out of our schedules. It can also be the state of mind in which we actively experience life in the midst of our busyness. As we live our daily lives, we can contemplate or meditate continuously on some thought or image in our minds.

> "It's nice to be at peace with you. It's fine with me to be close to you."
>
> —"Peace With You," by Ten Shekel Shirt (from *Breathe*)

Meditation as a state of mind is very similar to having a song or jingle stuck in your head all day (except not so annoying). Scriptural words or images get "stuck" in your mind and stay with you throughout the day. The constant presence of these words and images keeps your energy focused on God, enabling you to take a more peaceful and prayerful approach to what may be an otherwise hectic life. However you practice meditation, it requires you to take time out of your schedule to be in communion with God—to rest your voice and still your heart and mind to listen for God's voice. Meditation offers the kind of peace talked about in the line from the song by Ten Shekel Shirt (above). It is the kind of peace we find only when we are in the presence of God, and we know we are fine.

SOUL TENDING

Practicing meditation can be as simple as choosing a simple phrase, such as "God is good," upon which to meditate. Spend time in silence, considering God's goodness. Then, take some time in the quiet to think about how good God has been to you. Listen to what God might be saying to you about God's goodness (or what God might be saying that confirms God's goodness. You may want to write about your reflections or insights.

- Commit to thirty minutes each day this week to spend in meditation.

- Meditate daily on a challenging situation that you are facing in your life. Keep a journal to record your reflections and write about your experiences.

- Memorize an inspirational phrase, Scripture, or song lyric, and weave it into your thoughts for a week. Listen for God's voice as you play the phrase over and over in your heart.

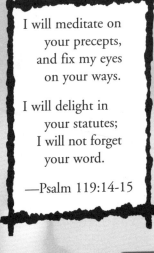

I will meditate on
    your precepts,
    and fix my eyes
    on your ways.

I will delight in
    your statutes;
    I will not forget
    your word.

—Psalm 119:14-15

Stillness and Silence

I'll Have Silence With That

Food is satisfying. We feel its effects in a full
stomach, increased energy, and improved mental
focus. We expect to eat three meals a day plus snacks.
None of us likes to go too long without a bite to eat,
something to fill ourselves up. Inspirational writer
Morton Kelsey sees a correlation between this
physical need for food and our spiritual need for
silence. He says that as the body needs regular intake
of food to sustain health, the soul needs regular
periods of silence in order to thrive.

We know that, as a general rule, the human body
can only survive three days without water and three
weeks without food. Although there are not similar
statistics for the amount of silence needed for survival,
the wisdom of our faith—from Ecclesiastes 4:6,
"Better is one handful with quiet than two handfuls
with toil, and a chasing after the wind," to Mother
Teresa, "The more we receive in silent prayer, the
more we can give in our active life"—illustrates the
value and need for silence in our lives. For many of us
silence tends to be a lot like eating our vegetables,
they may not be the best tasting thing on the menu
but they provide nourishment and energy in ways that
candy bars can't.

18

Silence Scares Me!

Silence can be frightening. One young person said, "I don't know what to do with silence. I always have music or the television on, even if I'm alone and have no one to talk to." Silence is so rare for many young people that finding oneself in the midst of silence can be uncomfortable. In the car, in an elevator, at the mall or in the gym, music and noise are a constantly part of the soundtrack to our lives.

Writer Dallas Willard challenges his readers to consider the inner emptiness that is present if they feel that they must always surround themselves with noise. For some making noise might be a habit, for others music may be a passion, and for others sound may be a way to block out inner thoughts or the still small voice of God. If noise is simply a habit, then one has a wonderful opportunity to explore the depths of stillness and silence. Silence may be a welcome change from the frantic pace and volume of daily life. If the music and busy-ness and constant chatter of the day is an intentional way to shut out inner thoughts and doubts, then experiment slowly with times and places of stillness and silence. It may be that there is peace and calm and healing in the silence just waiting for you.

> Better is one handful with quiet than two handfuls with toil, and a chasing after the wind.
>
> —Ecclesiastes 4:6

19

God Can Be in the Silence

The experience of the prophet Elijah illustrates beautifully the comparison of one's physical need for food to one's spiritual need for silence. In 1 Kings 19 we read that Elijah has angered Queen Jezebel, who has threatened to kill him. He flees from her and pleads with God to take his life. But instead an angel of the Lord waits upon Elijah instructing him twice to eat and drink, "He got up, and ate and drank; then he went in the strength of that food forty days and forty nights to Horeb the mount of God" (1 Kings 19:8). There at Mount Horeb, nourished and sustained physically, Elijah encounters God in the "sheer silence":

> [The Lord] said, "Go out and stand on the mountain before the Lord, for the Lord is about to pass by." Now there was a great wind, so strong that it was splitting mountains and breaking rocks in pieces before the Lord, but the Lord was not in the wind; and after the wind an earthquake, but the Lord was not in the earthquake; and after the earthquake a fire, but the Lord was not in the fire; and after the fire a sound of sheer silence. When Elijah heard it, he wrapped his face in his mantle and went out and stood at the entrance of the cave. Then there came a voice to him that said, "What are you doing here, Elijah?" (1 Kings 19:11-13)

God is always present, awaiting our attention. But it is in those moments when we have attended to our physical and spiritual needs that God can speak clearly to the deepest parts of our soul asking, "What are you doing here?"

20

Befriending the Silence

For centuries the breath prayer has existed as a way to connect with God. For some it is a way to befriend the silence; it gives a person something to do as he or she begins to experience holy silence. As you repeat the prayer, its words eventually blend into the silence so that you can be open to hearing what God might say. You can choose your own breath prayer and then repeat it over and over in rhythm with the inhale and exhale of your breath. First, choose the name for God that is most comfortable to you, such as Father or Mother, Comforter, or Lord. Second, choose a simple phrase that summarizes what you may need from your relationship with God right now. You might choose a line from a song or a verse of Scripture, as long as it is not too wordy. (You want to fit all the words on your inhale and exhale, and you don't want to hyperventilate!) Or you could use something like, "Be with me, God"; "Jesus, help me follow you"; "Spirit, give me strength"; "Gracious God, fill me with love"; or "Guide me, Savior."

> The more we receive in silent prayer, the more we can give in our active life.
>
> —Mother Teresa of Calcutta

During moments of silence breathe deeply in and out as you begin to breathe your prayer to God. Experiment with this prayer in different settings. You may want to sit in your room with palms upturned on knees to spend time in silence or enjoy stillness and silence before you read Scripture. Since most of us are used to being physically active, this may be challenging! Close your eyes to better concentrate on being still. Sit absolutely still without moving a muscle and become aware first of physical stillness. Then, move your focus onto your inward stillness. Close your time of prayer with a simple, "Amen."

> For God alone my soul waits in silence for my hope is from him. He alone is my rock and my salvation, my fortress; I shall not be shaken. On God rests my deliverance and my honor; my mighty rock, my refuge is in God.
>
> —Psalm 62:5-7

SOUL TENDING

Be warned that developing a practice and rhythm of stillness and silence in your life will change you. When you place yourself before God, open and undistracted, God will speak to you, call to you, and prompt you. This may be a slow process in which you grow to appreciate and long for these moments of silence in your day. Or you may find that God has been patiently waiting for this opportunity to speak a specific word to you.

- Find a place where you can be by yourself in silence. Read Isaiah 43:1–5a, substituting your own name for "Jacob" and "Israel" in verse 1. Get comfortable and take a few deep breaths. Then read the personalized verses from Isaiah over and over, slowly. Picture yourself resting in God's hands or loving embrace. Imagine that God is speaking these words directly to you.

- Designate a period of time when you will "fast from words." You may not be able to remain totally silent the entire time, but see if you can focus on staying as quiet as possible. If you must speak, choose your words carefully. Remember these words from Ecclesiastes 5:2: "Never be rash with your mouth, nor let your heart be quick to utter a word before God, for God is in heaven, and you upon earth; therefore let your words be few."

- Find a place where you can be still by yourself in silence. Set a timer for five minutes, then close your eyes, sit up straight, and relax into the silence. You might want to begin with a prayer like, "O God, be with me now." Don't try to make anything happen. When distracting thoughts come, refocus on the silence or repeat the prayer.

- Make time each day to pray your breath prayer. You could designate certain times of day (for example, when you awaken and just before you go to sleep), or certain actions (for example, every time you brush your teeth), or an amount of time (for example, set a timer for five minutes, as above).

Discernment

Choices, Choices

We are all called upon to make numerous decisions every day of our lives. In some cases, little is at stake and decisions are easy: What do I wear today? Do I raise my hand to answer the teacher's question? Other situations are more difficult: Do I tell my best friend that I am angry at her? Do I break up with my boyfriend or girlfriend? Some decisions might be easier to make if we did not have to worry about biblical instructions such as God's command not to steal (Exodus 20:15) or Jesus' command to love one another as ourselves (Matthew 22:39). But regardless of the circumstances, how we make our decisions says a lot about who we are and about our relationship with God.

Tools for the Task

Often, what it most difficult about decision-making is not knowing how to evaluate the options. If you think now about healthy and helpful ways to make decisions then you will be prepared when difficult decisions arise. Imagine a toolbox that contains tools you might need to make good decisions. Be sure to include in your decision-making toolbox the following: Think through the possible outcomes; talk with a family member, friend, or spiritual director; pray; write about the decision and the possible consequences in a journal; use Ignatius of Loyola's process of discernment.

Discernment: Making Decisions With God's Help

God has given us the means to make most choices on our own, but sometimes a decision is so complicated that our need for God's help is obvious. Many choices flow naturally out of who we understand ourselves to be. For example, "As a person of faith, I will not spread rumors, tell lies, or abuse my body." But what about being in a relationship with a friend who does those things? Other decisions can be equally complex: How does one know which college will be the best fit? How does one know when he or she is ready to get married? Which activities must get cut from a busy schedule?

Discernment is the process of making decisions with God's help. Centuries ago, Ignatius of Loyola, founder of the Roman Catholic order of Jesuits, suggested a process of discernment to guide people of faith through their decision-making. Here's a summary of Ignatius' process:

- Gather all the information you need to make a particular decision. This may include talking to persons who may have helpful insight into your situation or friends who know you well.

- Focus on one decision for a specific period of time. Write down any information that supports one option. Pray about it. Try to live as though you have already made this choice and pay attention to how you feel. Spend the same amount of time living with and praying about the other options. Compare your feelings toward different options.

- Make a tentative decision after considering your feelings toward all possible options. Do you feel more at peace with one choice? If so, offer that decision to God and know that you made the best possible decision you could make. If you still feel troubled, try an alternative choice or (if possible) postpone the decision until you know more and feel better about one particular choice.

Prayerful Decision-Making

Discernment is a way of making decisions that reminds us that we are not alone. God undergirds all that we do, and other people support us as we wrestle through complicated or troubling decisions. Look to the example of Jesus and other biblical figures to see how they made choices. In all our decisions, large and small, we should ask ourselves the following questions:

- Is a given choice consistent with who God calls me to be?

- How is the Holy Spirit informing my decision?

- Will a given choice help me become a more complete person?

- After spending quiet time with God about this decision, do I feel drawn toward one particular option?

Imagine the options available to the persons described below. Make a list of questions the persons below could consider in the discernment process. What tools could they use to make the best decision? Who might each of these young people go to for help?

- Maria is sixteen, pregnant, and concerned about her future. She must decide whether to keep the baby, have an abortion, or give the child up for adoption.

- Sam's mother's new job requires her to move to another state. Sam would like to stay in his current town to finish his last year of high school but doesn't want to be separated from his family.

- Anissa has been offered a job that might help her toward a future career. Taking the job, however, would mean working on Sundays and missing worship and church activities.

None of us knows what decisions we will have to make in the future; but as followers of Jesus, we do know certain things about ourselves. The statements below are true for all believers though truly believing them about ourselves can take time. These truths should affect every decision we make.

- I am a child of God.

- God wants me to be content.

- God created me to do good in the world.

- I can do all things through Christ who strengthens me.

SOUL TENDING

- Talk to your parents or other significant adults in your life about difficult decisions they have had to make. Find out how they made these decisions and talk to them about Christian discernment.

- Make a list of the big decisions that you expect to make in the next ten years. How could you begin the process of prayerful decision-making now?

- Read the following Scriptures each day this week: Psalm 73:23-24; 109:105; Romans 12:2; James 1:5. What does each one say about discernment?

- Talk to God about any decisions you are currently struggling with and use the process of discernment oulined on pages 25–26.

27

Honoring the Body

Many of us take our bodies for granted. We don't tend to notice the miraculous work of our organs and systems until we get sick or injured. Then we may marvel at how the body can heal itself. We inhabit the physical self—our one body, mind, and spirit—yet many of us think of ourselves in separate parts: I think (mind), feel and connect to God (spirit), and move or act (body). Yet God created us to be whole selves and desires that we be healthy physically, spiritually, and mentally.

In Clay Jars

In 2 Corinthians 4:7-10 Paul describes our bodies as clay jars:

> But we have this treasure in clay jars, so that it may be made clear that this extraordinary power belongs to God and does not come from us. We are afflicted in every way, but not crushed; perplexed, but not driven to despair; persecuted, but not forsaken; struck down, but not destroyed; always carrying in the body the death of Jesus, so that the life of Jesus may also be made visible in our bodies.

Clay jars in Paul's world were handmade, unique, and functional. Yet they were also fragile and prone to cracks and would shatter when dropped. We like to affirm that we are God's beloved creations, unique and gifted for a specific vocation. But many of us do not like to dwell on the fact that we are also fragile.

Today we have found alternatives for those fragile clay jars. We buy water in plastic bottles and have it pumped directly into our homes. But we have not yet found a way replace those vulnerable parts of ourselves that can break from misuse or abuse. As much as we would like to hide our cracks, it is often through our flaws and fragility that Jesus can be most visible to those around us.

Defiling the Temple of God

In an outrageous act of trust and grace, God created our fragile human bodies as temples of God.

> Do you not know that you are God's temple and that God's Spirit dwells in you? If anyone destroys God's temple, God will destroy that person. For God's temple is holy, and you are that temple. (1 Corinthians 3:16-17)

It is easy to forget that we are "God's temples." All of us sometimes act in ways that harm our bodies, minds, and spirits. We make choices each day to either honor our "temples" or hurt them. We can stretch and exercise or become too comfortable and stagnant in front of the television. We can honor the gift of sexuality in committed relationships or harm one another by exploiting it or using it to exert power over another person. We can protect our bodies from the lasting effects of drugs and alcohol or sacrifice our health by abusing those substances. Our bodies require the same care as a fragile clay jar and the same honor of the most beautiful and holy temple.

Go for Health: My Body Pledge

Studies show that mental, emotional, and physical health are closely linked. When our physical bodies are healthy, our minds and spirits benefit. Regular physical activity can help us stay balanced when we are under stress or are feeling down.

We all can take steps to claim and maintain our health. We can eat a healthy, balanced diet with lots of fruits and vegetables. We can follow a physical regimen that keeps our cardiovascular system strong and our brain alert. We can abstain from abusing harmful substances. We can carefully think through all our choices, asking, "Will this help me be healthy? Am I honoring God in me if I do this?"

Write a pledge about how you will honor your body. For example, "I will try to eat five servings of vegetables each day," "I will make an effort to stop smoking," or "I will exercise for thirty minutes three times a week to build muscle and maintain a healthy weight." Put your pledge in a stamped envelope and address it to yourself. Exchange envelopes with someone you trust and mail the letters to each other in one month as a reminder of the pledge you made.

SOUL TENDING

"Honoring the body" looks different as we age and move into different stages of life. Children run and play for hours a day getting the exercise they need and their parents are responsible for putting healthy meals in front of them to eat. As we age we have more responsibilities that fill our days and more options about how we will eat and take care of ourselves.

• Take a moment each morning to honor your body by saying the following affirmation: "I am a child of God. God made me beautiful and good."

• Keep a food diary for one week, writing down everything you eat. At the end of the week, think about your diet. How healthy is it? How could you commit to healthier eating?

• Keep a journal about your relationship to your body. What do you do to stay fit and healthy? How are you in partnership with the God who made your body? Think about the gift of health. How can you work to stay healthy?

- Pray about giving up behaviors that have a negative effect on your health. Seek support from friends, parents, or a recovery program to battle any addictions.

- Meditate on how your emotional and spiritual health are linked to your physical health.

- Do online research about a subjects that pertain to your personal struggles with staying healthy—for instance, marijuana use, sexually transmitted diseases, eating disorders, or maintaining an exercise regime.

- Look directly into a full-length mirror for five minutes each day this week. Observe God's wonderful creation before you. If you like what you see, thank God. If you do not like what you see, pray that God would show you how special and wonderfully made you are. Talk to a trusted friend or mentor about ways to love and care for your body.

Devotional Reading

The Dream Assignment

Imagine being in school and, amid all of your reading, homework, and term papers, your teacher hands you a novel with these instructions: "You don't have to finish this book. There will be no report or test. Just find a quiet place, start wherever you like, and read slowly and carefully. When you come across a word, phrase, or sentence that is interesting to you, stop and think about it. Do this same thing every day for a week."

Wow! You could forget about finding the main point, identifying the climax, and labeling the protagonist and antagonist. You wouldn't have to worry about diagramming sentences or stress about deadlines.

A Different Kind of Reading

But who really has the luxury of reading like that? In our busy world, many people prefer reading chunks and snippets to curling up with a good book. Students often skim or read just enough of an assigned text to get a good grade on the test; many adults grab a newspaper and glance at the latest headlines on their way out the door; many people are so infatuated with technology that, instead of reading for leisure, they hang out at their favorite wireless hot spot and surf the Internet while talking on a cell phone or listening to an MP3 player. Reading is often something we do to find specific information or to kill time hoping that something interesting will keep our attention for a few minutes.

It is tempting to approach devotional reading with the same mindset. Sometimes we read the Bible in hopes of finding information to support our point of view. Sometimes we seek comfort or guidance during a particularly difficult time. And other times we read out of a sense of obligation so that we can check "devotional time" off our to-do list.

But devotional reading requires a different mindset. While most Bibles conveniently include subheadings that tell us when certain stories and passages start and end, the Bible isn't written like a newspaper or a website. There are no flashy headlines to grab us, no banners or pop-up windows competing for our attention. Devotional reading helps us sense how the Spirit is working in us and reveals God's love for us. Reading spiritually requires discipline and focus.

Absorbing the Words

Devotional reading provides not only a purpose but also a method. The goal in devotional reading is not to answer who? what? when? where? or why? The goal is to find God in the words. Devotional reading gives the reader permission to slow down and truly listen to what God is saying through

> Come before the Lord and begin to read. Stop reading when you feel the Lord drawing you inwardly to himself. Now, simply remain in stillness. Stay there for a while.
>
> —Jeanne Guyon (1648–1717)

the text; it invites the reader to be mindful of those things that the Holy Spirit brings to his or her attention. Influential devotional writer and mystic Madame Guyon (see the quote above) instructs devotional readers to come to the Lord quietly and humbly, absorbing the words on the page.

Devotional reading is not limited to the Bible and devotional books. The work of ancient and contemporary theologians and even novelists may help us set our hearts and minds on God.

A theology professor once confessed that as a young adult she thought the history of Christianity skipped from Jesus and the apostles to her and her local church. Then she read about the church's rich history and discovered the ancient church mothers, fathers, and saints of the church, such as Teresa of Avila and Saint Augustine. She not only increased her knowledge but also found friends and soul mates for her faith journey.

SOUL TENDING

Choose a selection written by a historical saint or a favorite devotional writer. Say a brief prayer asking the God to reveal the Holy Spirit as you read. Read the passage slowly. Do not skim for a main point but look for God. Rest on certain words or phrases that speak to you. Do not panic if your mind wanders. Continue to pray and listen for God's voice. The point is not how much material you cover but how much time you take.

This type of reading may feel forced or difficult at first, but you may eventually find the practice natural and refreshing. Continue experimenting with devotional reading, listening for God's unique word for you.

• Research a particular saint of the church at a library or on the Internet; then make his or her writings part of your devotional reading.

• Commit to reading the same short devotional reading every day for a week. Record each day's insights in a journal

• Select a devotional book and ask a friend or mentor to read it with you. Discuss your experiences and discoveries.

Chastity

Chastity is not a common word in our culture, nor is it a terribly popular one. What comes to mind when you read the word *chastity*? Monks locked up in monasteries praying in sackcloth? a strict standard of purity and abstinence? In a culture where complex relationships are broken and mended in thirty-minute sitcoms and barely dressed men and women sell everything from underwear to cars, is chastity even realistic?

Chastity Isn't

A better understanding of chastity will help us as we struggle with the challenges of friendships, romantic relationships, and physical intimacy and how they affect our spiritual formation. First, chastity is not synonymous with celibacy, which means to abstain from sexual relations or marriage. Rather, chastity means letting go of the "I want" and "I must have" mentality that often drives our emotional and physical relationships. Imagine a relationship in which one person is totally absorbed in it, allowing it to consume his or her thoughts, time, and energy. At the beginning of a new relationship this constant attention to the other person and desire to be with him or her all the time is a normal reaction to our hormones, infatuation and giddiness. But when these feelings cause a person to neglect her other relationships or cause him or her to focus on the other person at the expense of his or her own well-being, that normal reaction has evolved into an unhealthy relationship.

Secondly, chastity is not a difficult burden forced upon us to keep us from enjoying love and intimacy. Instead it is an intentional effort to keep God at the center of all relationships. Chaste persons see God in one another, surrender self-centeredness in relationships, and do not try to control a relationship or own another person. Persons practicing chastity do not eliminate love, contain their desire for love, nor avoid physical intimacy, but they prayerfully aim to put God at the center of each relationship. In doing so, they make love the center of their relationships. Chastity means viewing every relationship (romantic or platonic) and sex as God's good gifts and learning how best to receive, care for, and share those gifts with others.

In 1 Thessalonians 4:1-8, Paul tells us how we ought to respect and care for one another:

> For this is the will of God . . . that each one of you know how to control your body in holiness and honor, not with lustful passion, like the Gentiles who do not know God; that no one wrong or exploit a brother or sister in this matter, because the Lord is an avenger in all these things, just as we have already told you beforehand and solemnly warned you. For God did not call us to impurity but in holiness.

Our bodies, holiness and the care of our brothers and sisters in Christ are all connected. Caring for our bodily needs requires attention to God's will for us. We also have a responsibility to make sure that those with whom we are in relationship honor their bodies as well. If our physical relationships do not honor one another's health and boundaries then we are exploiting one another and dishonoring God.

Chastity Is

The virtue of chastity is a way of life, a call to consider carefully and prayerfully how you will care for both your spirit and body and the spirit and body

of anyone with whom you are in relationship. Different people practicing chastity may choose differing levels of emotional and physical intimacy in relationships. According to *The Catholic Encyclopedia*, the practice of chastity "springs from the dignity of human nature." When making decisions one must view all persons as children of God, worthy of the utmost respect and care.

In our culture pure and truly intimate relationships are not the dominant form of interaction. Many relationships are short-term and only skim the surface of intimacy. In romantic relationships, practicing chastity is often difficult. Hormones and peer pressure can get the best of people. Sex is a gift from God, and it is good; but it can also be abused and harmful to us when we do not put God at the center of our relationships. Practicing chastity can give us balance and help us stay within our boundaries.

Read the story below about Alice. How is she practicing or not practicing chastity?

Alice is a seventeen-year-old young woman who began dating at age fourteen. She started dating Tony when she was a freshman and he was a senior. They saw each other on Wednesday and Sunday nights at youth group and then would hang out with his friends after football games on Fridays. They usually studied together or went to a movie on Saturdays. They had much in common but broke up when he left for college. She didn't find out until after he left that her friends were hurt about how little time she had spent with them.

Alice met Dylan at church camp where they were both junior counselors. They knew they would only be together for a couple months before school started again, so they spent as much time as they could together. Often their late night talks ended with a lot of kissing and touching. Alice didn't know if what they were doing was OK, but by the time she started to ask herself serious questions about their actions, camp was almost over. She didn't want to bring it up and ruin a great summer.

Now Alice is interested in Gary, with whom she works after school at the pet store. They have gone out a couple times this month. They can't go out much more than that because Gary always goes out with his friends on Friday nights. But he said he would like to meet her friends, and she invited him to come to youth group. They talk a lot at work; and they have been honest about past relationships, doubts, and fears. Alice thinks she would be OK talking with him about how comfortable she is with physical intimacy, if they continue to date.

Can you think of situations that you and/or your friends have been involved in that have been similar to Alice's? How could practicing chastity help us consistently have godly, healthy relationships?

SOUL TENDING

• Pray and write about your love life. Do you have a steady boyfriend or girlfriend? Are you dating? How might practicing chastity affect your relationship? Have an honest discussion with your boyfriend or girlfriend about levels of intimacy and boundaries and how can your relationship be pure and centered on God's love.

• Ask a trusted adult if he or she would talk with you, openly and honestly, about intimate relationships and chastity. Ask the adult to talk about his or her boundaries and how they were established.

• Answer these questions in your journal:

  † What word or words would you use to describe a dating relationship? to describe sex?

  † What words would your parents choose? your best friend? Your youth minister or campus minister?

  † How are these descriptions similar to or unlike what we learn from Scripture?

• Evaluate your relationships to see if God is at the center of each of them. Pray several times daily for each relationship you are in. Pray

that God would be the foundation upon which the relationship was built and that purity and dignity would be priorities.

Fasting

Editor's note: The object of fasting as we speak of it here is not to lose weight or punish oneself. The rigorous and strict abstention from food for extended periods of time as a form of weight loss, diet control, or penance can be both psychologically and physically damaging. It you are dealing with issues of self-worth that lead you to any type of eating disorder, please seek the help of a parent, counselor, minister, or physician.

What Is Fasting?

Fasting, abstaining from food accompanied by prayer and meditation, shows up throughout Scripture. In the Old Testament, the Jewish Queen Esther commands all Jews to observe a three-day fast in preparation for her plan to save the people (Esther 4:16). In the Acts of the Apostles (9:9), Saul (who later becomes Paul) reacts instinctively to his blinding experience with the risen Christ on the road to Damascus by fasting.

As the church grew, the regular practice of fasting continued among the early Christians. An anonymous document known as the *Didache*, or "The Teachings of the Apostles," from the first or second century, directs followers of Jesus to continue the regular practice of fasting on Wednesdays and Fridays (unlike the Jewish observance of the fast on Mondays and Thursdays).

John Wesley, the founder of Methodism, followed the tradition of the early church and continued the spiritual practice of fasting on Wednesdays and Fridays throughout most of his adult life. Wesley believed that one can observe the fast in three ways: abstaining from food, abstaining from particular foods (such as meat), or

39

abstaining from rich or pleasant foods (such as sweets or desserts). Wesley believed that fasting is an instituted or required means of grace but also a practice that has the potential to be abused by those seeking something other than a deeper relationship with God.

Why Do We Fast?

Fasting is the abstention completely from one's normal daily intake of food. But fasting as a Christian practice is not restricted to food. Fasting can also be the abstention from things that keep us from focusing on our relationship with Christ, such as watching television, surfing the Web, or engaging in the latest gossip. (Sorry, abstaining from homework is not an option. Nice try.)

Abstention in this form may be a much safer option if you are, because of medical reasons, unable to abstain from food. The object of the fast is to free time and energy normally spent focusing on our worldly needs to focus our time and energy on our spiritual needs through practices such as prayer, meditation and contemplation, and reading the Bible.

Observing the fast helps us to focus in times of struggle or decision, as well as times of deep spiritual or biblical study. When I am faced with a big decision or dealing with a particular issue concerning my faith, I find observing a fast helpful to focus my time and energy on prayer and meditation. A pastor I know, who has a tough time observing the fast, was inspired to persevere when the youth he led in a small group Bible study all decided to fast with him to enrich their Bible study. They would begin fasting after dinner the night before a meeting and break their fast by dining together at a local restaurant following the Bible study.

How Do We Fast?

In the passage from Matthew on page 42, Jesus provides us with clear instructions as to how we should observe our fast. Our fast is practiced before and for God and never for the attention of others. This directive does not mean that you must keep your fast completely secret. Letting those people close to you know about your fast spares them potential worry and gives them the chance to support your endeavors through prayer.

Jesus also says to his followers to "put oil upon your head and wash your face" when fasting. His command means that as one observes the fast, one should continue one's daily routines of cleaning and grooming. Jesus does not want us to look rough just to publicize our fast. Let the fast be a time of joy and an opportunity to grow closer to God.

> Fasting should never be practiced for weight loss. Your health should never be compromised while fasting. If you have problems with your self-image or are struggling with an eating disorder, fast from something other than food, such as television, talking on the phone, or a bad habit.

How Long Should I Fast?

Set realistic goals for yourself as you observe the fast and start slowly by abstaining from one meal or one daily habit. John Wesley observed the fast from sundown the day before until dusk on the day of his fast; for him, this constituted an entire day. The goal of going one day a week without food or a part of our daily routine is realistic for some. For others, fasting may need to be less frequent.

Remember that if you abstain from food during your fast, you should drink plenty of fluids like water or juice. Side effects you may experience during a fast from food include a growling stomach, hunger pains, headaches, and bad breath. Also be aware that, as you observe your fast, you should not engage in any form of strenuous activity or exercise. If you are involved in any type of sport or extracurricular activity that requires this type of activity, observe your fast on days you do not practice or play. Choose days that help you stick with your commitment.

> "And whenever you fast, do not look dismal, like the hypocrites, for they disfigure their faces so as to show others that they are fasting.... But when you fast, put oil on your head and wash your face, so that your fasting may be seen not by others but by your Father who is in secret, and your Father who sees in secret will reward you."
>
> —Matthew 6:16-18

SOUL TENDING

• Consider persons in our world who are genuinely hungry due to a lack of resources. How can fasting help us better understand or meet the needs of the malnourished? Organize a group fast for this purpose. For instance, you and your friends might give all the money you would normally spend on fast food in a given month to hunger relief. During this time you could also study the plight of hungry persons in the world.

42

- Journalist Catherine Marshall writes about God's calling her to fast from her habit of criticism. Fast from at least one bad habit for a week and write in a journal about it, using these questions:

  † What was most challenging about fasting from this bad habit?

  † Did you find anything positive to replace this habit and help keep your focus?

  † Was prayer involved in your fast? If so, for what did you pray?

  † Will you go back to practicing this habit, or did your fast help you overcome it?

- Use a concordance to search Scripture for the word *fasting*. While reading each passage, answer these questions:

  † When and why do the people in these Scriptures observe the fast?

  † What is the result of their observance of the fast?

  † What do these passages have to say about my experience with fasting?

Keeping the Sabbath

The Meaning of Sabbath

The word *sabbath* is derived from the Hebrew word shavat, meaning "to cease and desist." This definition gives us some idea of what sabbath is all about. So does Scripture. Exodus 20:1-17 and Deuteronomy 5:1-21 command God's people to observe of sabbath on the seventh day of the week as a holy day. In Exodus God explains the sabbath as both a covenant between God and the people of Israel and a day of rest that they Israelites should observe faithfully.

Sabbath and Our History as God's People

As the Jewish faith developed, rituals for keeping the sabbath also developed and evolved. Today, practicing Jews observe sabbath from sundown Friday until sundown Saturday. According to the Jewish calendar, this time from Friday evening to Saturday evening is the seventh day of the week.

By contrast, the early Christians decided to observe sabbath on Sunday to recognize Christ's resurrection and the work of the Holy Spirit on Pentecost. In the Gospels, Jesus and some of the Pharisees (those who believed in the strict observance of the Law both inside and outside of the Temple) clash over how they understand the sabbath. Jesus taught that the sabbath was created for people to worship the Lord, not to discourage one from doing God's work. For Jesus, doing the work of the Lord meant healing the sick and caring for the poor in spirit. The Pharisees disagreed. They considered sabbath a time to cease totally from all physical labor, regardless of the purpose of the work.

As the Christian church developed, so did Christian education and corporate worship, which are important ways in which people continue to keep the sabbath today. As the Christian church, we keep the sabbath by setting aside our regular schedule and resting from the busyness of our lives. We attend Sunday school, and in worship we embrace and feast upon God's presence in our lives.

Keeping Time Holy on the Sabbath

Sabbath need not be limited to Sunday; it can be observed any time of the week. As with other disciplines, such as fasting, sabbath is not just about what we don't do but about what we choose to do with our time. In breaking from the schedule of our everyday lives, we free up time to truly rest, to embrace wholly our relationship with God, and to feast on God's presence in our lives. There is a sense, then, that we can somehow reclaim that time we spend on unfocused busyness to make it holy. Rabbi Abraham Joshua Heschel, in his book *The Sabbath*, echoes this idea about regaining our time and making it holy when he calls the sabbath, "a palace in time which we build."

But resting on the sabbath does not mean sitting on the couch for twenty-four hours. Rather, the sabbath can be a day to dust off that old model airplane, make time for the yoga class, or talk to an old friend for an hour on the phone. The sabbath is a time to step away from other obligations and reconnect with the passions, gifts, and relationships that God has given us.

Sacrificing on the Sabbath

Numbers 28:9-10 explains that an extra offering or doubling of offerings is required for the people of Israel to properly keep the sabbath. This idea of sacrificing things on the sabbath runs contrary to the lengthy to-do lists we often cram into Sunday afternoons before the week begins again.

SOUL TENDING

- Take some time to reflect on these questions about keeping the sabbath:

  † What do you cease on the sabbath?

  † How do you rest on the sabbath?

  † What do you embrace on the sabbath?

  † How do you feast on the sabbath?

- Marva J. Dawn suggests that the main benefit of keeping sabbath is that we cease trying to be our own god and let God care for us. List the benefits you now receive from keeping the sabbath. What might be holding you back from enjoying the full benefits of holy rest and play?

- Before going to bed this Saturday night, read Exodus 31:13-17 and reflect on the busyness and work of your week. Make a list of ways you will refrain from working and truly rest on Sunday. Pray that God will give you the strength and ability to rest. On Sunday night write down your thoughts on what, if any, difference your Saturday night preparation made in helping you keep the sabbath.

- Observe a time of sabbath during the week if Sunday is too busy with church activities. Spend this time doing the things you love and thank God for the gift of sabbath.

- Organize a sabbath retreat. Invite a mentor to come and lead your group in prayer and devotion. Spend an entire weekend basking in God's love.

Forgiveness

People aren't perfect. You can't always count on others to treat you fairly. And believe it or not, they are not depending on you to always have their best interests at heart either. It can be startling to think how many people have crossed your path since you crawled out of bed this morning. With each interaction there is the chance of disappointing someone or having your own feelings hurt. In any given day you may feel happy, sad, gracious or frustrated. In those moments of impatience it is easy to respond to others with a quick-tongue or knee-jerk reaction that causes more harm that good.

We might not even be conscious of how we hurt others. We might just let the jabs that come our way roll right off our backs. Forgiveness for the little scrapes and scratches in our day-to-day relationships might happen almost automatically. But sometimes something happens that wounds clear to the core of our being. Sometimes our words and actions severely hurt others. Then there are awful tragedies, real crimes, and horrible injustices, when forgiveness becomes an issue of faith!

Forgiveness as the Heart of God

Forgiveness is at the heart of God. God yearns to forgive, aches to forgive, and hurries to forgive. Forgiveness proves that the power of love is stronger than anything that might separate us from God. Forgiveness can be a powerful and transformational experience. Being forgiven frees the forgiven from the shame, heaviness of heart, and self-hatred that ultimately cut them off from God and those they care about most. What if one were bullied, held by police for no reason, or raped? What if a close friend were killed by a drunk driver?

Our gut reactions may be anger, a desire for revenge or retaliation. But the challenge of discipleship is to move beyond these instinctive human reactions, to rely on God, and to allow forgiveness to permeate own hearts so that we might offer forgiveness to those who have hurt us.

Me? Forgive Me?

Sometimes we can't stand to face the one who stares back at us from the mirror. Sometimes assurances of God's forgiveness don't sink in. Even efforts by others to help us forgive ourselves fall short. Our responsibility for a broken relationship may be too painful to admit. But it is precisely these wounds that God wants to take and heal. God wants to replace self-hatred and emotional paralysis with acceptance and love.

In our worst moments we feel unlovable and pull away from those who love and care for us. Isolated, we exacerbate feelings of unworthiness and refuse to claim the love and acceptance that could heal us. Forgiveness can break this cycle, bringing us back into relationship with those we have hurt, restoring our relationship with God, and drawing us closer to the abundant life that God desires for each of us. Forgiveness can purge our gut-level anger and knee-jerk desire to get even. A new attitude—a new impulse to forgive—comes to life in us as we realize God's forgiveness in our hearts.

We also have the responsibility and privilege of offering the saving grace of forgiveness to those who have wronged us. We can choose to alienate and sever ties with those who have hurt us or seek reconciliation. A world that trusts the power of forgiveness to transform and give new life would look a lot like the Kingdom of God that Jesus sought to bring to earth.

Jesus teaches that we are forgiven even as we forgive. Forgiveness is in our best interest! It's part of the faithful life of a believer. Peter was trying hard to get it right when he asked Jesus, "How often should I forgive?" (Matthew 18:21). But for Jesus how many times one forgives doesn't matter. What matters is making forgiveness a habit.

SOUL TENDING

• Often when we struggle with forgiveness, we look for loop holes to excuse our need to forgive, such as:

  † comparing ("It's not as bad as what she did.")

  † minimizing ("It's not that bad.")

  † defending ("He had it coming.")

  † justifying ("I had no choice. He deserved it.")

  Do you see yourself looking for and using these loop holes?

• Commit to surrounding yourself with friends who consistently seek to offer and receive forgiveness. Be a witness of God's forgiveness for one another and for the world.

• Before you go to sleep each night this week, take a brief inventory of your day. From whom do you need to seek forgiveness? For what do you need to ask for forgiveness?

• Three times this week, read about Jesus and forgiveness in Matthew 9:2-8; Matthew 18:21-35; and Luke 7:36-50. What does Jesus teach about forgiveness? Write down your reflections about how you could be a more forgiving person.

Bible Study

Did you know that in Greek there are five different words with similar but distinct meanings that are all translated "love" in English? Or that there are two different accounts of creation in the book of Genesis? Have you noticed that the phrase, "this occurred in order to fulfill what was spoken by the prophet" is mentioned several times throughout the Gospel of Matthew? Are these just interesting facts to impress your friends, or do they tell us important things about ourfaith and who God is?

A Story of Us

The Bible tells the story from beginning to end of God's making the world in love, the world's rejection of God, and God's continual effort to restore God's relationship with creation. The Bible is the story of us. It contains our past, present, and future. It consists of history, poetry, and stories, but is much more. The Bible is a message from God. Through Bible study, God reveals truth and wisdom to us.

These revelations are relevant to our biggest existential questions—who are we and why are we here?—and our everyday interactions with friends and families. Studying Scripture bares truth and guidance for personal struggles and sheds light on ills in our society and the world. Learning methods for Bible study can only increase the richness and depth of love and reverence for Scripture.

A Controversial Book

In almost every denomination, church, and even Christian family, disputes go on about how to read and understand the Bible. Is the Bible the only source for wisdom? Is every word of the Bible inspired, or God-breathed, and without error? Is the Bible entirely consistent throughout the Old and New Testaments? How historically accurate is the Bible? As you grow in your faith and encounter these questions, you will find it helpful to have some idea of where to look in our sacred Scriptures for information that will help you in your search for answers.

Knowledge and Discipleship

2 Peter 1:3 says, "His divine power has given us everything needed for life and godliness, through the knowledge of him who called us by his own glory and goodness." Peter's second letter teaches that knowledge is essential to discipleship. Stanley Hauerwas, a theologian and professor of Christian ethics, insists that "discipleship is required for the right reading of Scripture." A Christian's faith journey is a cycle of study, reflection, and action that helps him or her to be a faithful disciple of Jesus Christ. There is value in studying the Beatitudes (Matthew 5:3-12; Luke 6:20-23). But when you have walked with one who is poor or felt the pain of a friend who is meek, then the Scripture comes alive; you are called into deeper discipleship and the Scripture calls you back for greater study and understanding. The cycle sends us forth into the world and calls us back again to the nurture and calling of the Scriptures.

Just as you are a student of history, algebra, chemistry, or English, you are also a theologian, a person who studies God. Bible study can be an exciting part of your faith journey as you begin to understand the roots

of many Christian traditions, make sense of your
spiritual experiences, and practice your reasoning
skills when wrestling with the hard issues of life.

SOUL TENDING

Many tools are available to assist you in your study and
understanding of the Bible. Bible dictionaries, concordances, and various
commentaries on the Bible are available in libraries and bookstores. You
can also ask your pastor for recommendations or ask to borrow
resources from her or his office.

• Using the tools discussed, spend time this week finding more
  information about a biblical topic that you have questions about.

• Check your Bible or go to your pastor's office, church library, or
  local library and look for maps of ancient Palestine during Jesus'
  lifetime. Find Bethlehem, Jerusalem, and Nazareth. Get to know the
  land in which Jesus lived and walked.

• Skim a Bible concordance. What topics included surprised you? Which
  seem lacking? Choose a topic to research and spend time studying it.

• Find a study Bible with footnotes and commentary. Read Proverbs 2:1-
  15. Then read the footnotes. How do the footnotes and commentary
  help you better understand this Scripture? Read the passage again.
  What do you understand better or differently now?

• Read your favorite Bible passage in several different Bible
  translations, such as the New International Version, New Revised
  Standard Version, and the Contemporary English Version. What
  differences and similarities do you notice? Are the differences
  among translations helpful or confusing? What new insights do you
  gain from reading these different versions?

Self-Denial

Athletes do it. Musicians do it. Artists do it. Our parents even do it for our benefit. We see forms of self-denial all around us. Yet self-denial is among the most difficult of Jesus' teachings. When we deny ourselves, we give up something or choose one path instead of another. Often this involves avoiding something we enjoy or crave or selecting a path that is more difficult than the alternative. Self-denial reminds us that following Jesus is a way of life, not a one-time decision. One book of early Christian teachings, *The Didache*, begins, "There are two ways: one of Life—one of Death. There are great differences between these two ways" (*The Didache*, 1.1).

> If we do not continually deny ourselves, we do not learn of Him. ... If we do not take up our cross daily, we do not come after him, but after the world, we are not walking in the way of the cross, we are not following him.
>
> —John Wesley,
> Sermon 48

Choosing Christ Instead of Ourselves

In his epistles, the apostle Paul told Christians to change their lives and deny themselves for Christ's sake. For early Christians, this meant fighting the temptation to participate in aspects of the dominant Roman culture that were incompatible with the Christian faith. Christian thinkers throughout history have taught self-denial as a way to stay focused on God in a sometimes hostile environment. Christians today may find that self-denial is an effective way to overcome the allure of consumerism.

53

It's Not Easy!

Every decision we make is an opportunity to practice self-denial. We can choose to deny ourselves pleasure, convenience, recognition, or fortune. The trick is to determine which acts of self-denial will bring us closer to God.

For instance, walking instead of driving a car gives one an opportunity to take in God's creation and, as a form of exercise, honors the body. On the other hand, denying oneself by walking backward instead of forward probably doesn't have the same spiritual benefit.

Self-denial also means knowing when to stop. God does not want us to give up so much that we jeopardize our health or deny ourselves so many of life's pleasures that we are miserable. Setting unreasonably high expectations for ourselves can also be the result of excessive pride.

Knowing how to practice self-denial requires prayerful discernment. The messages we receive from the media and popular culture lead us to desires that compete for our attention. Even simple, healthy acts of self-denial can end up being very trying.

> If any want to become my followers, let them deny themselves and take up their cross and follow me.
>
> —Mark 8:34

Self-denial is difficult for several reasons. First, discerning what is the right decision is not always easy. Sometimes a choice may appear appealing, yet it can be destructive. As Christians we have the ability to choose wisely even when the choice is difficult. Romans 2:15 tells us that God's law is not foreign to us, but that it is woven into the fabric of our very being. Something deep within us echoes God's yes and no and tells us right and wrong.

Second, we cannot do everything. At times we take on too much, and we pay the price. When we think we can do it all, we are guilty of the sin of pride. When we are unable to deny ourselves, we risk harming ourselves and others. Maybe we are unable to honor a commitment; maybe we get so frustrated that we blow up at someone; maybe we just get so overwhelmed that we burn out.

Third, focusing on those things that God wants us to focus on can be very difficult. The media sends us several messages that tempt us and compete for our attention. When we simplify our lives and deny ourselves that which we don't need or which isn't good for us, we can better focus on God's intentions.

Fourth, self-denial can be difficult when the choice is very clear, but we recognize that God is calling us to do something that is not pleasurable or enjoyable. In these situations we get a small taste of what Jesus meant when he told us to deny ourselves and take up our crosses. (See Mark 8:34.) The way of Christ often requires us to make sacrifices.

But There Is Joy

By becoming Christians, each of us said to God and to the worlds: "Not myself, but Christ." God asks us to affirm this choice every day. The more we live out this commitment to Christ, the more joyful we are.

Jesus practiced self-denial. He was tempted to do many things that were contrary to God's will (Matthew 4:1-11; Luke 4:1-13), but drawing on his knowledge of God and of Scripture, Jesus was able to overcome these temptations. In his life we see the model for self-denial.

Facing death, Jesus denied his own will, praying, "Not what I want, but what you want" (Mark 14:36). And in the ultimate act of self-denial, Jesus laid down his life for our behalf.

> Then Jesus was led up by the Spirit into the wilderness to be tempted by the devil ....
>
> Again, the devil took him to a very high mountain and showed him all the kingdoms of the world and their splendor; and he said to him, "All these I will give you, if you will fall down and worship me." Jesus said to him, "Away with you, Satan! for it is written,
>
>> 'Worship the Lord your God, and serve only him.' "
>
> —Matthew 4:1, 8-10

SOUL TENDING

- Reflect on how Jesus practiced self-denial. Think about his life, and record two or three biblical passages that give examples of this practice.

- What does it mean to pray, "not what I want, but what you want"?

- How, by resisting temptation, could you deny yourself and take up your cross?

- Spend time each day this week in prayer surrendering yourself to God's will. Keep a list of all the ways that God has used you as a result of offering yourself so completely to God.

- Commit to giving something up this week that would benefit someone else. Give up your telephone time to go to the grocery store for your family; resist the temptation to gossip and instead say nice things about everyone with whom you come in contact; or volunteer at a nursing home, a food pantry, or a shelter instead of going out on the weekend.

- As you wake each day this week, pray the words of Jesus, "not what I want, but what you want" as a daily act of submitting to God's will.

Lectio Divina

Lectio divina. So what's that? Some kind of strange-sounding disease? The Latin term for an insect? No—it's something much better than that! *Lectio* means "reading," and *divina* means "spiritual" or "holy." Spiritual reading—the name itself is a clue that this way of reading is clearly different from the way we might read a textbook, sports magazine, or favorite website.

In this approach to the Bible, we are looking for something more than information. We are seeking formation and transformation. We aim to be renewed by God (Romans 12:2) and to have the "same mind in us that was in Christ Jesus" (Philippians 2:5-8). *Lectio divina* is a reflective and prayerful kind of reading. It is about quality, not quantity. It is about going deeper, not about covering a lot of territory.

In a way, instead of our reading the Bible, we open ourselves and allow the Bible to read us. Have you ever read a verse in the Bible that seemed to be written just for you, that applied directly to your life? Hebrews 4:12 vividly describes the power of God's Word: "Indeed, the word of God is living and active, sharper than any two-edged sword, piercing until it divides soul from spirit, joints from marrow; it is able to judge the thoughts and intentions of the heart."

Allowing the Bible to Read Us

Lectio divina goes back to ancient Jewish traditions of meditating on Scripture. You can see this practice in Psalm 1:1-2: "Happy are those who…delight…in the law of the Lord, and on his law they meditate day and night." In the sixth century Saint Benedict refined this practice for monastic communities; and in the centuries since, both Roman Catholics and Protestants have widely used this method of reading the Bible.

Perhaps this way of reading Scripture is already familiar to you. When something in Scripture catches your attention, you stop reading and think about it some more. In the same way you chew your food, you process and reprocess this spiritual food until it is more fully digested by your heart and mind.

When you practice *lectio divina*, you will want to choose a short passage of Scripture, maybe four to eight verses. *Lectio divina* follows the following process:

- First, invite God to speak to you through Scripture and prepare yourself to listen.

- Read the Scripture through once, then again, slowly.

- Read it aloud a few times. Listen for one word or phrase that attracts you or seems to stand out from the rest of the words.

- Reflect on the word or phrase that sticks with you. "Chew" on the words for awhile.

- What is God trying to say to you through this word or phrase?

- Pray about what God has said to you in this Scripture. Are you thankful? sad? angry? Do you feel guilty? enlightened?

- Rest and simply enjoy God's presence.

- Record any insights you receive during this time.

Marjorie Thompson, a prominent writer in the area of spiritual formation, says, "The manner of spiritual reading is like drinking in the words of a love letter or pondering the meaning of a poem. It is not like skittering over the surface of a popular magazine or plowing through a computer manual. We are seeking not merely information but formation."[1] When pondering a love letter or reading a poem one can enjoy the written word without feeling pressure to "get it." While *lectio divina* reuqires focus, patience, and practice, the goal is simply to spend time with Scripture and with God.

Sixteenth-century mystic Teresa of Avila reminds us to slow down and enjoy reading Scripture and to be grateful for each bit of wisdom it imparts. "We should accept with simplicity whatever understanding the Lord gives us," she says, "and what he doesn't we shouldn't tire ourselves over. For one word of God's will contains within itself a thousand mysteries." So immerse yourself in Scripture. Appreciate the mystery and open yourself to be formed by God's Word.

SOUL TENDING

- Read the same passage of Scripture for five consecutive days, using the steps of *lectio divina*. You might be surprised by the many ways that the same Scripture can speak to your life. Suggested texts: Psalm 63:1-8; Jeremiah 1:4-9; Habakkuk 3:17-19; Matthew 5:3-12; Colossians 3:12-17.

- Use a concordance to find Scriptures related to an interesting topic. Read a different Scripture passage about this subject daily, using *lectio divina*. Write down your insights.

[1] Reprinted from *Soul Feast: An Invitation to the Christian Spiritual Life* by Marjorie J. Thompson. © 1995 by Marjorie J. Thompson. Used by permission.

Giving Thanks and Praise

What prompts you to praise God? Is it a natural wonder, special person, accomplishment, piece of music, work of art, faithful testimony, or problem solved? How do you praise God? with dance? with trumpet and cymbals? with your mouth? (See Psalm 150).

Looking to God

We can't praise if we don't look to God. We can't praise if we don't recognize God's hand in our lives. We can't praise until we accept and receive God's love. When many of us would be tempted to question or curse God, Mary, Jesus' mother, chose to see God's hand at work and bless God not only for God's blessing in her life but for God's presence and strength through history.

And Mary said,
   "My soul magnifies the Lord,
      and my spirit rejoices in God my Savior,
   for he has looked with favor on the lowliness
         of his servant.
      Surely, from now on all generations will
         call me blessed;
   for the Mighty One has done great things for me,
      and holy is his name.
   His mercy is for those who fear him
      from generation to generation.
   He has shown strength with his arm;
      he has scattered the proud in the thoughts of
         their hearts.
   He has brought down the powerful from
         their thrones,
      and lifted up the lowly;

he has filled the hungry with good things,
and sent the rich away empty.
He has helped his servant Israel,
in remembrance of his mercy,
according to the promise he made to our
ancestors,
to Abraham and to his descendants forever."
(Luke 1:46-55)

Once our eyes are open to God's awesome love and
power in our lives, we give thanks and turn our gaze
toward God. We love and adore God. We cherish
God's steadfast love in Christ. We treasure God's
tolerant ever-present Spirit. We praise and bless God.
Recognizing God's majesty and greatness and
expressing delight is a spiritual practice. We can fix
the attitude of our souls to be in adoration and praise.
It is good to celebrate God's nearness and love.

A Matter of Focus

Thanksgiving is all about what God has done for
us. Gratitude means taking nothing for granted. If
faith is our response to God's presence in our lives,
then expressions of thanks are at the heart of our
spiritual lives. In Luke 17:11-16, the Gospel writer
recounts the healing of a leper:

On the way to Jerusalem Jesus was going through the
region between Samaria and Galilee. As he entered a
village, ten lepers approached him. Keeping their
distance, they called out, saying, "Jesus, Master, have
mercy on us!" When he saw them, he said to them,
"Go and show yourselves to the priests." And as they
went, they were made clean. Then one of them,
when he saw that he was healed, turned back,
praising God with a loud voice. He
prostrated himself at Jesus' feet and thanked
him.

The man with leprosy recognized his healing as a sign of God's love. He said, "Thanks!" and his relationship with God rose to a new level. He wasn't just healed—he was saved! Our own spiritual lives can be enriched by recognizing and naming the blessings in our lives. Giving thanks for the small blessings like a note from a friend just when we needed it or the extravagant acts of grace of healing and forgiveness reminds us of our dependence on God.

Praise focuses on God's greatness. Psalm 145 is an example of pure praise. Praise doesn't analyze, demand special favors, or greedily ask God to "do it again." Praise declares God's faithfulness, love, and compassion. Praise honors God for who God is and claims utter dependence upon God's grace, mercy, and awesome love.

SOUL TENDING

- Explore the Scriptures. Look for a phrase, verse, or passage that moves you to give thanks and praise. Memorize it. Use this Scripture to center yourself for your daily prayers.

- Set aside a time of fasting to help turn your gaze toward God. Spend your fast celebrating God's mighty acts by praising and giving thanks. This might be an especially meaningful way to celebrate Advent or Lent or to prepare for the sacrament of Holy Communion.

- Old Testament priests offered sacrifices to God in the morning and evening. Begin each day by offering praises from your lips. End each day with prayers of thanksgiving.

- Adopt a "fussy" plant that is utterly dependent on your nurturing care. Let your time tending the plant be a reminder to give thanks and praise for all that God is to you.

Prayer From a Repentant Heart

I can still hear the voice from a preacher at a youth camp I attended, "Repent today in case you die tonight!" The implied message from this well-meaning preacher was that unless we repented of our sins right at that moment, we would not be granted eternal life with God, nor merit God's love. I later learned that God's love for me did not depend on my immediate actions nor my fear of going to hell, but on my humble heart accepting and receiving God's love.

Not From Fear but From Love

God does not call us to repent out of fear for our eternal future. We are called to repent out of our love for God and our desire to have an intimate relationship with God through Jesus Christ.

Repent is not a word we hear often in our culture. A friend does not typically call us in the middle of the night to say, "I need to repent." We do not go to our parents to confess, "I am repentant." But "to repent" simply means to turn and go in the completely opposite direction. When John the Baptist calls out, "Repent, for the kingdom of heaven has come near" (Matthew 3:2), he is calling people to turn from their sin and begin a new life. In the same way, we are called to repent today. Jesus calls us to turn from our sin and begin our lives again in him. The friend who calls in the middle of the night may be calling to say that she has decided to leave an abusive relationship; she is ready to turn away from it—to "repent" of it. We may go to our parents to confess we have lied and turn away from the deceit that is hurting the relationship.

Psalm 139 tells us just how well God knows us. God knows our insides and outsides, our comings and goings, our ups and downs, our thoughts near and far.

O Lord, you have searched me and known me.
You know when I sit down and when I rise up;
　　you discern my thoughts from far away.
You search out my path and my lying down,
　　and are acquainted with all my ways.
Even before a word is on my tongue,
　　O Lord, you know it completely.
You hem me in, behind and before,
　　and lay your hand upon me.
Such knowledge is too wonderful for me;
　　it is so high that I cannot attain it....

Search me, O God, and know my heart;
　　test me and know my thoughts.
See if there is any wicked way in me,
　　and lead me in the way everlasting.
(Psalm 139:1-6, 23-24)

God's intimate knowledge of us helps us understand repentance. Because we are so well known, we ought not be afraid to come to God with a repentant heart.

How to Turn

Although the message is not explicit in the text, the writer of Psalm 139 teaches us how to repent and how to live a life of faith. Verses 23-24 teach us how to pray, asking God to search every part of our lives and take away all the sin that would separate us. When we have sin in our lives, we are not as close to God as God longs for us to be. Praying from a repentant heart means recognizing that God wipes away our sin and leads us in a completely new direction. When we claim God's forgiveness, we are freed from our sin— free to walk side-by-side with Jesus on our journey of faith. This closeness to Christ keeps us always attuned to his will for our lives.

SOUL TENDING

- Pray Psalm 139, reading it very slowly and pausing after each section or thought. Meditate on each phrase and ask God to examine each area of your life and remove the sin that separates the two of you. What thoughts or feelings arise? Do you feel free from your sin? Are you intimidated by how well God knows you?

- Memorize Psalm 139:23-24 and make it the beginning of your daily prayers.

- Using a concordance, find where the words *repent* and *repentance* appear in the Bible. Study these Scriptures to gain a fuller understanding of what Jesus means when he calls us to repent.

- Each time you pray, commit to asking God to examine and clean out your heart.

66

Seeking and Granting Forgiveness

Maya spent years trying to be a Christian, but she finally gave up. "The forgiveness thing was too tough for me," she explained. "Forgiving other people sounds good on paper; but in real life, there were simply some people I could not forgive." Maya is right. Living as a forgiven and forgiving person is a difficult part of being a Christian. Yet one of the beauties of the Christian faith is the simple fact that Jesus says, "Forgive, and you will be forgiven; give, and it will be given to you" (Luke 6:37-38). All of us have moments when we sin in thought, word, and deed. We sin by doing certain things and by leaving certain other things undone. Therefore, it is important that we know both how to seek forgiveness and how to grant forgiveness to others.

As We Forgive

When Jesus taught his followers how to pray, he made clear the connection between receiving God's forgiveness and forgiving others. "Forgive us for doing wrong, as we forgive others," Jesus says in Matthew 6:12 (CEV). Some may have more trouble accepting forgiveness than forgiving someone else; others may ask for and accept forgiveness while holding on to a grudge about a past wrong done to them. Jesus teaches us that we must receive, accept, and grant the forgiveness that is offered by God through Jesus Christ. As we allow that forgiveness to flow through us, we are transformed by the love of God.

67

A Right-on Parable

We live in a society where people who are angered by the actions of others often respond by going to court instead of by offering forgiveness. But Jesus had something else in mind when he told the parable of the unforgiving servant (Matthew 18:23-35):

> For this reason the kingdom of heaven may be compared to a king who wished to settle accounts with his slaves. When he began the reckoning, one who owed him ten thousand talents was brought to him; and, as he could not pay, his lord ordered him to be sold, together with his wife and children and all his possessions, and payment to be made. So the slave fell on his knees before him, saying, "Have patience with me, and I will pay you everything." And out of pity for him, the lord of that slave released him and forgave him the debt. But that same slave, as he went out, came upon one of his fellow slaves who owed him a hundred denarii; and seizing him by the throat, he said, "Pay what you owe." Then his fellow slave fell down and pleaded with him, "Have patience with me, and I will pay you." But he refused; then he went and threw him into prison until he would pay the debt. When his fellow slaves saw what had happened, they were greatly distressed, and they went and reported to their lord all that had taken place. Then his lord summoned him and said to him, "You wicked slave! I forgave you all that debt because you pleaded with me. Should you not have had mercy on your fellow slave, as I had mercy on you?"

Imagine the terror and panic the slave must have felt when the king threatened to have him and his family sold into slavery. Then a few moments later he surely fell to his knees overcome with relief that his debt had been forgiven. But as he left the king's presence, he must have already begun thinking about how he will provide for himself and his family. As he ponders his dilemma, he just so happens to come across a fellow slave who owes him money—eureka! The memory of his own forgiveness and relief are forgotten as he callously sends his fellow servant to jail. Sometimes we become so focused on our own needs that we forget the love and grace we have received and become unable to share it with others. Our challenge as disciples of Christ is to love with imagination and forgive generously.

A Radical Alternative?

Some people refuse to act in revenge and retaliation. An organization called Murder Victims' Families for Reconciliation even has a mission to abolish the death penalty. These people, all of whom have family members who were murdered, are putting their energy into working for policies and programs that reduce the rate of homicide and promote alternatives to violence. Reconciliation means accepting that you cannot undo the murder but that you can decide how you want to live afterward. Wow! Think of losing a loved one, then having the strength to forgive the murderer.

Hear the words of Luke 23:33-34a, "When they came to the place that is called The Skull, they crucified Jesus there with the criminals, one on his right and one on his left. Then Jesus said, 'Father, forgive them; for they do not know what they are doing.'" Even as he was dying, Jesus was able to forgive those who had pierced his hands with nails, cast lots for his clothing,

69

and watched as he suffered on the cross. Even then he forgave. Jesus doesn't ask us to do anything he didn't already do, and his death makes possible our own forgiveness.

SOUL TENDING

- Look at some different translations of Matthew 6:12. How do the different wordings clarify the meaning of this verse?

- Pray the following prayer each night this week and notice the transformation in your view of people and situations.

  Almighty and merciful God, you made us. You love us. You forgive us. We are grateful for what you have given us, yet still we fail to follow the path you have set before us. We do not live out of the fullness of your love. Instead we say and do things that hurt others. We allow our words and actions to be governed by prejudice and misunderstanding rather than by your justice and righteousness. We are selfish and unsympathetic when you call us to "take up our cross." We are afraid to speak out for truth and not sure we can handle the consequences of discipleship. And so we ask your forgiveness. Give us the strength to reflect your love through our own loving lives. Let us forgive others as we know we need to be forgiven. All things are possible in you. Amen.

- Commit to seeking forgiveness from whom you need it or granting forgiveness to those who need it from you.

- Read Matthew 6:12 daily. Commit these words to memory and allow them to shape your relationships with God and others.

- Write a prayer asking God for forgiveness. Ask God for the strength to seek forgiveness from others and to grant forgiveness to others.

Stewardship of Household Economics and Money

The fact that Jesus said more about money than about any other temporal subject is convincing evidence that he considered one's relationship to money a spiritual issue. Remember that he was speaking to people in a simple society where land was the primary valued asset. What would he say to us today who live in a world of high technology, great material wealth, and seemingly endless ways to spend money?

Need or Want

In the course of a day we name dozens of things that we "need." We tell our parents we *need* new socks and extra highlighters for class. We talk with our friends about the new CDs or gadgets we *need*. As the seasons we change we realize that we *need* warmer clothes or new shoes. And, of course, we *need* to make sure we have three meals a day ... plus dessert and snacks in between. But if we were pause each time we said the word "need" and ask if "need" is really the appropriate word, how many times could we honestly answer "yes"? How many times would we have to replace "need" with "want" or "covet"? How can we draw clear lines between what we truly need and what we just want?

Start With the Basics

Jesus actually taught about money and material wealth more than any other subject. The Scriptures below give us a sense of Jesus' attitude toward wealth and possessions:

> Then he looked up at his disciples and said: "Blessed are you who are poor, for yours is the kingdom of God.... But woe to you who are rich, for you have received your consolation." (Luke 6:20, 24)

> And he said to them, "Take care! Be on your guard against all kinds of greed; for one's life does not consist in the abundance of possessions." (Luke 12:15)

> "No slave can serve two masters; ... You cannot serve God and wealth." (Luke 16:13)

Jesus does not mince words. An attachment to money and stuff can be dangerous.

Bigger Barns

Being responsible with money and possessions is difficult for persons living in a prosperous nation. We don't have to look far to find someone with greater material wealth than we have. Many people fall into the trap of comparing themselves to movie stars and professional athletes who boast multimillion-dollar homes, numerous cars, and stock portfolios worth more than the operating budget of a small city. "I don't really have that much," we tell ourselves. "It won't hurt to buy one more DVD or one more pair of jeans." Will we never be satisfied?

Jesus' parable of the rich fool (Luke 12:13-21)

aptly illustrates the consumer culture in which we live. As you read this parable, think of the storage facilities that pop up in every community, the storage units that sit in people's driveways, and the closets, garages, and attics overflowing in so many homes.

> Someone in the crowd said to him, "Teacher, tell my brother to divide the family inheritance with me." But he said to him, "Friend, who set me to be a judge or arbitrator over you?" And he said to them, "Take care! Be on your guard against all kinds of greed; for one's life does not consist in the abundance of possessions." Then he told them a parable: "The land of a rich man produced abundantly. And he thought to himself, 'What should I do, for I have no place to store my crops?' Then he said, 'I will do this: I will pull down my barns and build larger ones, and there I will store all my grain and my goods. And I will say to my soul, Soul, you have ample goods laid up for many years; relax, eat, drink, be merry.' But God said to him, 'You fool! This very night your life is being demanded of you. And the things you have prepared, whose will they be?' So it is with those who store up treasures for themselves but are not rich toward God."
>
> —Luke 12:13-21

Rethinking Possessions

Richard Foster, writing about simplicity, gives some practical ideas about not getting sucked in by consumer society and focusing instead on "treasures in heaven" (Matthew 6:20). Here are some of his suggestions:

- Buy useful things, not trendy things.
- Reject addictions.

73

- Regularly clean out your closets and give away what you don't use.

- Avoid being wooed by commercials.
- Enjoy things instead of possessing them.

- Deepen your awareness of God's good creation.

- Turn from whatever distracts you from your goal.

Giving Out of Our Abundance

If we compare our own lives to that of an Afghan refugee, Salvadoran orphan, or a homeless person in Chicago, we have to admit that we have it pretty good—at least in terms of material wealth. One of the gifts of having enough (or more than enough) is that we can then give from our abundance to others. As Paul wrote in 2 Corinthians 9:8 and 11a, "And God is able to provide you with every blessing in abundance, so that by always having enough of everything, you may share abundantly in every good work.... You will be enriched in every way for your great generosity."

Giving helps others and makes the giver feel good. God calls us to give as an act of worship and an outward expression of God's love.

Tithing and Regular Giving

When we consider that everything we have comes from God, we should want to give back to God a portion of what God has so generously given us. Tithing is the practice of giving ten percent of what we have to God in obedience to God's command in the Old Testament (Leviticus 27:30-33). Offerings are gifts given above and beyond our tithes, not out of obligation, but out of worship and gratitude.

When a person sets aside a portion of what he or she earns or receives, that person is saying, "God is more important in my life than money or possessions." Placing one's cash or a check into an offering envelope can be a powerful act of worship that frees one from being enslaved to one's possessions. "I put God first," says one young person. "Even if there's another bill I can't pay in full, my tithe goes to God's work. It's so little compared to all that God has done for me."

SOUL TENDING

- Divide a sheet of paper into three columns labeled, "Real Treasure," "Nice to Have," and "Can Live Without." Make a list of the things (material and otherwise) that you value, use a lot, want to have, or spend a lot of money on. Then place each of these items in the appropriate column. Which of these could you do with out? Which do you truly need?

- Imagine that a great fire or flood is moving toward your home. You have ten minutes to gather together a few things before you must evacuate. What will you take? Make a list; then write about why each of these items is so important to you.

- Spend fifteen minutes each day this week thanking God for all your treasures.

- Each day this week, read the story of the rich young man who came to Jesus. Matthew 19:16-24. Imagine what might have happened in that young man's life after his encounter with Jesus. Try writing a new ending to the story.

- Keep track this week of every expense, including even the smallest amount spent. As you look at where your money goes, pray that God would show you how to use your money faithfullly. Then create a budget that reflects your insight.

- Think about your own life. When and how have you been "a cheerful giver"?

- Ask your parents or other significant adults about their giving practices.

Stewardship of Creation and Time

Called to Stewardship

A good steward is one who takes special care to use all things wisely. One can be a steward of money and use it well in saving, spending, and giving. One is a good steward of the earth when one cares for all aspects of God's creation and uses natural resources responsibly. Stewardship of time involves how one approaches every moment of one's life.

Brother Sun, Sister Moon

Twelfth century monk Saint Francis of Assisi, who has influenced many subsequent generations of Christians, lived in communion with nature. He found creative new ways to relate to different parts of creation: "Brother Sun," "Sister Moon," "Brother Wind," and "Mother Earth." These names were born out of the close connection Francis felt with nature. As God's blessed creation, Francis felt a kinship with God's other creations.

Often we tend to look at creation through the lens of science—reducing creation to numbers and formulas—or to look upon the wonders of the universe with awe. But both science and wonder keep creation at a distance. If we could see each animal, each rock, each body of water, each star, each galaxy, each microscopic organism as members of our family—as fellow children of God—we would live and interact with our environment differently. The threatened extinction of a species or ecosystem would become more urgent and personal.

Stewardship of the Earth

Genesis 1:26-31 tells us that God has created the entire universe and has deemed everything "very good":

> Then God said, "Let us make humankind in our image, according to our likeness; and let them have dominion over the fish of the sea, and over the birds of the air, and over the cattle, and over all the wild animals of the earth, and over every creeping thing that creeps upon the earth."
> So God created humankind in his image, in the image of God he created them;
> male and female he created them.
> God blessed them, and God said to them, "Be fruitful and multiply, and fill the earth and subdue it; and have dominion over the fish of the sea and over the birds of the air and over every living thing that moves upon the earth." God said, "See, I have given you every plant yielding seed that is upon the face of all the earth, and every tree with seed in its fruit; you shall have them for food. And to every beast of the earth, and to every bird of the air, and to everything that creeps on the earth, everything that has the breath of life, I have given every green plant for food." And it was so. God saw everything that he had made, and indeed, it was very good. And there was evening and there was morning, the sixth day.

God then entrusted this good and pleasing creation to humanity, giving us "dominion" over the earth and our fellow creatures. In his paraphrase of the Bible, *The Message*, Eugene Peterson translates dominion as "Take charge! Be responsible." Honoring both of these mandates can be difficult. For example, we certainly have taken charge of the coal buried deep within the mountains of West Virginia; but have we responsibly mined the coal and treated those who risk their lives to retrieve it?

Isaiah 24:4-5, may have been written thousands of years ago, but the prophet's words continue to ring true and help us understand how to be good stewards of God's creation today:

> The earth dries up and withers,
> > the world languishes and withers;
> > the heavens languish together with the earth.
> The earth lies polluted
> > under its inhabitants;
> for they have transgressed laws,
> > violated the statutes,
> > broken the everlasting covenant.

How we understand our dominion over the earth is one of today's most pressing theological questions.

Where Do You Stand?

In recent decades environmental issues have come to the forefront of our public consciousness. Familiarity with global climate change, ozone depletion, water pollution, and the effects of chemicals on the soil has increased significantly. Many major cities now provide curbside recycling. Yet Americans as a whole still consume at an unrelenting rate, landfills are overflowing, and several types of major pollution persist.

God gives each of us not only the gift of life but also the beautiful world in which we live. Taking action on behalf of one's physical environment can be an enriching part of one's spiritual journey.

Stewardship of Time

Just as God is present throughout creation, God is present in every moment. Thus carefully managing our time is as important as caring for our physical environment. We need to make time for prayer, Christian fellowship, and sabbath. We also need to eliminate those things that make poor use of our time.

SOUL TENDING

• Copy this prayer and put it in your purse or wallet. When you reach in to get out money or make a call on your cell phone, pause to pray:

> God of heaven and earth, help us see the true beauty of your creation. Teach us what it means to have dominion over the earth that you created for us. Give us the wisdom to care for the earth and make responsible use of our time

• Brainstorm ways to apply the "three r's of conservation" (reuse, reduce, recycle) in your daily life. Make a pledge to overcome one bad. For instance, if you drink one soda each day and presently throw the can in the trash, promise yourself that you will find and use a recycle bin for aluminum. Or if you have a habit of leaving the water running while you brush your teeth, be intentional about shutting it off in between rinsings.

• Reflect on the following questions and answer them in writing:

    † In what sense is my time no just my own, but God's?

    † How can I devote time each day to God?

    † How does my time management reflect my faith? How can I better use my time faithfully?

• Find an environmental group whether an on-campus club or national organization for whom you can volunteer.

79

Prophetic Witness

Are you puzzled, challenged, or even angered by what goes on in the world? Do you wonder why there seems to be such a huge difference between the world that God intended and the way things really are? Do you ever find yourself asking—even begging—God to intervene to change the course of history or to bring about peace, justice, and righteousness? Do you ever wonder if God is sending a message to our broken world through you?

"Thus Says the Lord"

In the Bible, prophets are those who speak God's Word about a particular situation. They are in tune with the events of their time—warfare, poverty, worship of false gods, and spiritual complacency—and they actively listen for and discern God's will. The perception that prophets "predict the future" is only partially true. Prophets articulate visions that often have implications for the future but, more importantly, have implications for the present.

In the Old Testament, the books written by and about the prophets are the second major portion of Scripture, following the Law. Prophets like Isaiah, Jeremiah, and Ezekiel called the people to follow God's Law, to have faith in God's salvation, to accept God's judgment, and to receive God's mercy. The prophets did this by making the God's word plain ("thus says the Lord") and by pointing out signs from God. Jeremiah spoke of a potter working with clay (Jeremiah 18:1-11), which teaches us that God shapes and molds us for a variety of purposes. Ezekiel witnessed a valley of dry bones that came to life (Ezekiel 37:1-14), a reminder that God can bring life out of death.

Two Evils and One Kingdom

Prophetic words are always vivid and stark—they get our attention! The biblical prophets spoke chiefly against two evils: the tendency to worship other gods and neglect of the poor. The prophets spoke to the complacent and self-sufficient, warning these people of coming disaster if they did not repent and change their ways. They spoke to people in exile, who had been driven from their homes, and assured them that God was with them.

Prophets of all ages envision a reality that is so different from what we know that we are forced to look and listen. Isaiah spoke of the wolf lying down with the lamb in his vision of the "peaceable kingdom" (Isaiah 11:1-9). In a world marred by war, violence, and conflict, God's vision for the world is given to us by prophets, and we are called to live into that vision.

Martin Luther King, Jr., was one such prophetic witness in the last century. He reminded people of the difference between their public profession (that "all are created equal") and their practice in regard to racial inequality. He called Christians to listen to the prophets of old. King paid homage to the Bible's prophetic tradition by citing one of his favorite Scriptures: "Let justice roll down like waters, and righteousness like an ever-flowing stream" (Amos 5:24).

Today's Prophets

Journalist Finley Peter Dunne famously said that the job of a newspaper is to "comfort the afflicted and afflict the comfortable." The same can be said about prophets. To those who are comfortable and complacent, prophets bring a warning. To those who are suffering and burdened, prophets bear a message of hope.

Someone once wrote to a North Carolina newspaper lamenting that so many people were quoting the Bible to condemn one another. The writer then offered the following teaching of John the Baptist to readers: "Whoever has two coats must share with anyone who has none; and whoever has food must do likewise" (Luke 3:11). This simple reminder of a common Bible verse served as a prophetic witness. Many people have more than one coat. Many others have none. Through this man's witness some were afflicted, others comforted.

Young persons have traditionally been at the forefront of the church's prophetic witness in the world. Youth and young adults often come to the Word of God with a freshness and can see clearly make connections between the Word and what is going on in the world. Listen to the prophets! And do not be afraid to speak boldly when you hear the Word of God calling upon you.

SOUL TENDING

- Who are the prophetic voices in your congregation and community? How can you show your appreciation to these persons?

- What issue in your community or in the world bothers you or keeps you awake at night? What would your community look like if God's vision for it were to become a reality?

- Read the Book of Amos this week. How is his prophetic voice a witness for you today? How will his words inspire you to act?

- How might God be calling you to speak up?

82

Singing From the Soul

Do you sing in the shower? How about when you're alone in your car? Do you shout along to your favorite songs in the car as if the road were your stage? Consider the special occasions that prompt singing: weddings, funerals, worship services, athletic events, military workouts. Think of other ways we use song: as a memorization aid or to get to sleep. Music is an integral part of everyday life. Somehow we express feelings with much more clarity and profundity when they are sung. In the same way, music has the potential to draw a person closer to God.

Finding Your Voice

Some people have beautiful singing voices. Others have a gift for playing one or more musical instruments. Still others can hardly carry a tune, have no idea how to strum a guitar chord, and are incapable of producing anything resembling a note on a trumpet or trombone. But when our songs are directed towards heaven, regardless of our natural ability or lack thereof, God hears only beautiful music. Consider Psalm 89:1, "I will sing of your steadfast love, O LORD, forever; with my mouth I will proclaim your faithfulness to all generations." The psalmist's first instinct, when overcome with God's glory, was to sing.

Brother Roger, the founder of the Taizé community in France, said that when the singing we do in worship lingers in our hearts during times of solitude, we are in true communion with God. We can experience this communion with God privately or amid hundreds of fellow worshipers. When we sing, our minds relax, leaving an openness in the soul where the human heart is free to lean in ever so closely to the heart of God. Additionally, Martin Luther suggests, God's Word takes root in us as we sing to God.

John Wesley, the founder of Methodism, in his "Directions for Singing" (which are still printed in the front of *The United Methodist Hymnal*) urges, "Have an eye to God in every word you sing.... Attend strictly to the sense of what you sing, and see that your heart is not carrried away with the sound, but offered to God continually." Wesley's advice doesn't apply only to church services, but also to the tunes we sing along to in our cars or bedrooms. Do we move closer to God when we join in and sing our favorite songs? Do we sense God's presence in the lyrics and melodies?

God's grace is available to us through song— through hymns, through secular and sacred music, and through the music we create ourselves. Listen for God in the music you listen to and sing along with and sing with joy the song that is in your own soul.

SOUL TENDING

- Select a favorite Psalm, possibly Psalm 150, and sing it over and over to a familiar melody. Allow the melody to sink in.

- Chant the song from Revelation 4:8b on one note: "Holy, holy, holy is the Lord God Almighty, who was and is and is to come."

- Commit to singing from the soul in church this Sunday. Pray the hymns and choruses as you sing them in worship.

- Write a song this week about your love for God.

- Throughout the week, listen for ways that God speaks to you through different kinds of music.

Speaking the Truth in Love

Do you ever "beat around the bush" or put up a "smoke screen" instead of speaking the straight truth? How many times have you walked away from a conversation wondering what the other person really had on his or her mind? How often do you say what you think somebody else wants to hear instead of what that person probably needs to hear? Do you ever get into trouble by saying one thing and doing something entirely different?

Imagine that it's December and a friend asks you to help recruit a day's worth of Salvation Army red kettle bell-ringers. You want to say yes to this good cause but really need to say no. You talk awhile to keep up appearances, offer a few excuses, and try to say no without really using the word *no*. You walk away thinking you've gotten away with a no. Then three days later, your friend calls and asks you for the names. You've got a problem—a spiritual problem.

Yes, Yes and No, No

James 5:12, echoing Jesus' teaching in Matthew 5:33-37, says, "Above all, my beloved, do not swear, either by heaven or by earth or by any other oath, but let your 'Yes' be yes and your 'No' be no, so that you may not fall under condemnation." Like the "red kettle" situation above, saying what will make us look good or avoid an uncomfortable situation is tempting. But often when we aren't upfront about what we think and feel, our actions will reveal our true intentions and the contradiction between what we say and what we do. When our tongue tries to help us make a good impression, we tend to get caught telling half-truths or talking gibberish.

We may have similar struggles in conversations with friends and family members about personal or moral issues. When we disagree with people close to us we have do decide whether to speak up for our values and beliefs or go along with crowd. We hold in tension concern for our relationships and concern for our moral and spiritual integrity. In the end, speaking the truth in love (Ephesians 4:15), with respect and compassion, edifies both the speaker and the listener.

> We must no longer be children, tossed to and fro and blown about . . . by people's trickery, by their craftiness in deceitful scheming. But speaking the truth in love, we must grow up in every way into him who is the head, into Christ from whom the whole body, joined and knit together by every ligament with which it is equipped, as each part is working properly, promotes the body's growth in building itself up in love.
>
> —Ephesians 4:14-16

Our story of redemption is the story of a loving God who makes and keeps promises. We follow a Savior who speaks truth that lights our way and guides our understanding. God calls us to make known this good news and to make God's love real in our world.

Plain and Honest

Language is a blessing from God and should be used to praise God and build up others with God's love. If we were to speak only in response to promptings from the Holy Spirit, then we might listen more and talk less. We would choose each word more carefully, pausing to think and consider our Christian Scriptures and tradition instead of carelessly blurting out our opinions. If we took more care in our conversations then we would be less likely to contradict ourselves or give people the wrong impression.

Paul's letter to the Ephesians tells us that "speaking the truth in love" is an important part of our being the body of Christ. What would Paul have to say to our culture, where sarcasm, flattery, and crude humor have become standard means of communicating? Even in our conversations with family, honest talk about disappointment and frustration is often replaced by sharp words, rolling of the eyes, and shrugged shoulders. Conversations with friends are too often peppered with slams and attempts at humor at the expense of someone's self-esteem instead of true expressions of love and admiration. By contrast, Paul in Ephesians encourages us to shun "trickery" and "craftiness" in favor of talk that builds up the body of Christ (Ephesians 4:14-16).

SOUL TENDING

- Consider what you might say in each of these situations:

    † You are out with friends and someone starts gossiping.

    † Someone asks you for a date, but you don't want to go.

    † A friend confronts you about your choice to avoid certain stores because of what you consider unethical business practices.

- Write a story for children about the difference between looking good and being good.

- Keep a "yes-and-no" log for two days. When was your "yes" a "yes" and your "no" a "no"? When did you use half-truths, sarcasm, or flattery?

Spiritual Direction

Whether learning to play the guitar, paint in oils, speak a new language, or perfect skateboard tricks, any new venture requires energy and commitment. Having a coach usually helps. The same is true of the spiritual life. If we feel ready to go deeper, learn more, and draw closer to God, we must make time to learn and grow in that endeavor. A spiritual director can help a Christian stay focused on God and mature in faith.

What Is Spiritual Direction?

Marjorie J. Thompson writes in *Soul Feast*, "Spiritual direction is basically the guidance one Christian offers another to help that person 'grow up in every way ... into Christ' (Ephesians 4:15). A spiritual guide is someone who can help us see and name our own experience of God."[1] The job of the spiritual director is neither to pass judgment on another's spiritual journey nor to tell the directee what to do to fix his or her problems. Rather, a good spiritual director is above all a careful listener who offers a safe space for the other person to look deeply at his or her spiritual walk and encourages the person to recognize and respond to God's presence in his or her life. Directors and directees often read Scripture and pray together.

What Would We Talk About?

To prepare for an initial meeting with a spiritual director, take an inventory of where you are on the spiritual path. For instance, you may say, "I go to

worship and campus fellowship, but I don't know how to pray. I would read the Bible, but it doesn't make sense to me. Yet I still feel that God is in my life." You need to be open, honest, and ready to talk about parts of your life that you may not usually reveal other people. You can trust your spiritual director to protect your confidentiality—whatever you say will stay between the two of you.

You may want to prepare for ongoing meetings by identifying important events in your life since the previous meeting. Where did you see God? How have you lived out your faith? Your director will know good questions to ask to help you put your life into perspective and may suggest spiritual disciplines for you to try between your meetings.

Tough Questions

Are there one or two questions that you would like to discuss with a spiritual director? These are not questions about whether you should go to a party or a movie on Friday night. These are questions that keep you up and night and that could cause you to change your major or your job. A spiritual director will struggle together with these questions; he or she will pause to listen to you and watch for the movement of God in your life.

SOUL TENDING

- Read Acts 8:26-40. How did Philip act as a spiritual guide for the Ethiopian eunuch? What traits did each of these men have that led to a positive spiritual encounter?

- Think about whether or not you are ready to enter into a relationship with a spiritual director. If you are, talk to your pastor or campus minister about possible directors at nearby retreat centers or churches. If your pastor or campus minister feels comfortable and equipped for the role, he or she might also be a good choice as spiritual director. An older man or woman, mature in the faith, may also serve in this role.

- Read John 3:1-6 each day this week as you reflect on finding a spiritual director. Remember that Nicodemus was a learned man of religion, yet something drew him to Jesus. How did Nicodemus show openness to Jesus? How did Jesus mentor Nicodemus in the faith?

- Pray aloud the prayer below.

- Who has served as a spiritual mentor or guide for you? Write them a thank-you letter this week and pray for them as you mail the letters.

Loving God, you know us better than we know ourselves. You understand that we want to be faithful to your call but sometimes get distracted. We have so many other things to think about! Yet we realize that, even when we forget you, you always remember us.

Gracious God, help us to make you a priority in our lives. If we need a spiritual director, help us seek and find someone to meet with who will listen to us and help us mature in faith. Walk beside us on our journey. In Christ's name we pray, amen.

[1] Reprinted from *Soul Feast: An Invitation to the Christian Spiritual Life* by Marjorie J. Thompson. © 1995 by Marjorie J. Thompson. Used by permission.

Living Simply

Do you overbook your days chasing here, there, and everywhere? Have you ever had to collect your scattered self so you could make an important decision? Do you let the stuff you own have control over your life? ever lay awak at night thinking about all you have to do? ever think about why your life is so full? ever wonder if it makes any difference at all? If this is you, simplicity must sound like an oasis in the desert of your frantic life.

But simplicity isn't a pill that promises to cure burnout and fatigue. It doesn't come from typing your schedule into a whiz-bang techno-organizer. It isn't a planner or a new way to multi-task. Living simply is not about deciding to get your life under control but about giving control of your life to God.

On the Inside

Many of us are so busy that we don't take the time to reflect on what controls our life. Christian discipleship requires that we regularly take inventory of what we treasure (see Matthew 6:19-21), whom we serve (see Joshua 24:14-15), who owns us, and what aspects of our life take up the most energy.

Jesus teaches us a great deal about wealth and priorities. His bottom line is about as simple as simplicity gets: seek God, trust God, and receive God. But following these simple instructions can be anything but simple in our complex world. We need to ask ourselves, how far are we from truly believing that God will take care of our basic needs? Do we trust God and gratefully receive God's gifts or do we get wrapped up in worry and trouble ourselves about what (and how much) we "own."

91

Clearing the Clutter

Simplicity means clearing away the clutter on the inside and outside, modifying how one feels about wealth, and changing the way one calculates one's worth. Clutter may include material possessions that one doesn't use or that one values for the wrong reasons. Clutter may come in the form of a desire for wealth or prestige that distracts us from our relationship with God and others. Clutter may involve all the things we take for granted and use irresponsibly, resources such as energy and water and paper. By reducing the clutter in our lives, we can focus more fully on what God calls us to do and make more of our resources (whether money and material possessions or time and spiritual gifts) available for people who truly need them.

SOUL TENDING

- Practice planned spending. Make a budget and stick to it. Pay cash (rather than using debit or credit cards) when you shop so that you feel the immediate impact of the money you spend.

- Part of living simply is understanding that God's provisions are gifts and are not ours to keep. Our spiritual ancestors freed God's gifts during the year of Jubilee (Leviticus 25:8-55). Celebrate a day of Jubilee by freely sharing your God-given riches with others.

- Visit the Alternatives for Simple Living website at *www.simpleliving.org* to find other practical ideas for simplifying your life.

Solitude

On My Own

For most people, a typical day provides few opportunities for solitude. When we wake up, someone else is in the house (or apartment or dorm room), whether a family member or roommate. Throughout the course of a day the bulk of our time is spent with other people. Either we are in conversation with someone, in line with several someones, driving to meet someone, or eating with someone else. While all this interaction can be exciting and enlightening, a lack of solitude—time to ourselves—can drain our energy and focus.

Jesus Sought Solitude

Before Jesus began his ministry, he spent forty days alone in the desert (Matthew 4:1-11). He again spent time alone before choosing his disciples (Luke 6:12). In Matthew 14:13, we read that, when he heard of the death of John the Baptist, Jesus "withdrew from there in a boat to a deserted place by himself." In his short ministry, people who wanted him to preach, teach, heal, and change their lives constantly surrounded Jesus. As a counterbalance to this sometimes frenzied activity, Jesus consistently went away to be alone.

Alone Is Not Lonely

Jesus and many others over the centuries have found that solitude is a necessary ingredient of a healthy spiritual life. To practice solitude is to designate time with God only. Prayer, journaling, and reading Scripture are all ways to spend quiet time with God. Some people go on silent retreats for days at a time. Others have a focused quiet time every day where they meet God in the solitude. The challenge for our culture today is for busy people who live constantly surrounded by other people to find the time and place for solitude.

If you're a person who likes to lie in bed for a few minutes after you awake but before you get up to start your day, you could designate this time as "God time." Take a moment to talk to God and hear what God is saying to you. Similarly, if it takes you a while to fall asleep at night, let those quiet moments be a time of solitude with God. If you run or work out by yourself, dedicate that time alone time with God. Find ways to build solitude into your already existing routine, even if it means staying an extra fifteen minutes in the bathroom to brush your teeth!

Just Be With God

A healthy spiritual life includes extended times set apart to be alone with God. Perhaps you are often the only one at home on Wednesday evenings. You might keep a weekly "appointment" with God in prayer, Bible study, journaling, or whatever helps you connect to God. On a nice day you could go alone to a park or on a rainy day to the library—any place where you would feel comfortable sitting silently with God.

SOUL TENDING

- Complete the following sentences for yourself: I like to be alone when ___. The hardest thing about being alone is ___. The difference between being alone and being in solitude is ___.

- Read Mark 6:30-32. When have you benefited from resting awhile or wished you had been able to go somewhere by yourself to do so?

- Many Native American tribes have a tradition of "vision quest" for young people, a time apart where a young person is alone in nature to ask for vision for the future. How might a similar tradition be an important part of the Christian spiritual journey?

- Make time to be alone with God. You could reflect on any of the following questions, and/or write in your journal, and/or pray: Where have I recently seen God? For what am I thankful? Is there any problem I need to turn over to God?

- Take time in solitude to read Scripture. Read slowly, stopping to meditate on what you are reading. Some good places to start: Psalm 139; Philippians 2:1-11; 1 John 4:7-21.

- Talk to your parents or friends about what you've learned about solitude. Ask if they feel a need for more alone time. How can you support each other to meet those needs?

- Commit yourself to ten minutes alone with God each day.

- Listen for the times when you hear God nudging you to go and be away from other people. As you attune your life to God's nudges, you will find that seeking quiet alone time becomes second nature.

Testimony

Jesus used two main teaching methods: storytelling and teaching by example. We know how we are to love others because of Jesus' parables and the way he reached out to love all people, even those on the fringes. But Jesus taught one message directly, without using metaphors or asking us to observe: Go and tell others about him. This practice is sometimes referred to as "testimony"—telling about our Christian experience. We learn from Scripture that testimony can take many forms.

Some believers tell of dramatic conversion experiences, like Paul on the Damascus Road (Acts 22:6-16; 26:12-18). Other Christians look back on a difficult time of life to discover that Jesus was present with them the whole time, like the disciples on the Emmaus Road (Luke 24:33-35). Still others' testimonies describe a faith handed down to them through faithful family members that has been growing in them since birth, like Timothy and his mother and grandmother (2 Timothy 1).

Beverly Burton is a professional storyteller. Her experiences growing up in a rural community left her with many memories that she often shares in her stories. Her stories describe a particular place and the people who lived there. Surrounded by grandparents, aunts, uncles, and cousins, Beverly can relate to Timothy. Recalling memories of events that involved some of these relatives, she tells stories that teach lessons of respect, responsibility, and love. Initially when telling these stories, Beverly didn't refer to them as her "testimony." But after reflecting on the way these experiences have molded her faith, she saw them differently. She is reminded of the faith of her

 grandmother and her mother, along with many others. In this way, she is able to recognize the same faith in her life that Paul saw in Timothy's.

A Collection of Testimonies

The Bible can be understood as a book that contains the testimonies of the spiritual giants that have gone before us. The testimony of Isaiah may inspire you. The faithfulness of Ruth may leave you in awe. Peter might give you hope when you feel beyond redemption. And Mary's story may give you the courage to say "yes" to the next step in your own journey.

God's grace has such an effect on us that we must tell our story. Our lives are testimonies to God's grace. When we tell our stories, we reveals a little more of the grand Christian narrative and may inspire or embolden others, whether believers or spiritual outsiders.

SOUL TENDING

- Our testimonies are not something we keep to ourselves. We have a great story to tell. Write your answers to the following questions as you consider how you can tell God's story to others:

    † What prevents you from giving a testimony?

    † What about your faith experience is most unique?

    † Besides verbally, how else might you tell your faith story?

- Write your faith story this week. Start with, "A time in my life when I felt close to God was ___" and add to it each day.

- Ask one of your parents, your pastor, or another person whom you respect to tell you about his or her faith story.

- Write or e-mail someone who has shaped your Christian faith. Express your gratitude for that person's testimony, telling him or her of its importance to you.

Sacraments

It happened the same way every time. Just after I acknowledged the judge and just before I started my routine, I would find my mom in the crowd to see her smile and give me the thumbs up. This ritual during every gymnastics meet was not extraordinary because it made my routines perfect or because it took away all my fears. The extraordinary thing was that my mom smiled and gave me the thumbs up no matter what the state of our relationship was. Proud, annoyed, excited, or angry, my mom always looked directly into my eyes and gave me the thumbs up.

Ordinary Made Extraordinary

Sacraments are simply the ordinary things we do through which God gives extraordinary grace. Through baptism, God conveys grace to allow us to begin our lives anew. In Holy Communion, God through Christ conveys saving grace and power over death. Thankfully the sacraments are not dependent on our faithfulness as a people or our worthiness as individuals. Baptism and Holy Communion are God's gifts to us—God's beloved children.

The consistency of unconditional love from my mom helps me understand the sacraments. God does not withhold the sacrament of baptism because there are hungry children in the world whom we have not yet fed. Instead God continues to work in people's hearts, bringing children to baptism to remind us through the sacrament that all persons are God's children worthy of love, safety, and care. Similarly, God does not deny anyone Communion until he or she is worthy but invites all to the table. As we

98

celebrate Holy Communion, we find God waiting for each of us, ready to reveal again God's power over death by forgiving our sins and showering us with grace.

The sacraments are not merely memorized words and rituals to help us imagine events in the distant past but new and real experiences of God. They are tactile and gustatory ways of experiencing God. We feel the water and taste the bread and wine. In these seemingly ordinary acts, God is present in the most extraordinary way.

Baptism

Through baptism we are adopted into the family of God and brought into the covenant God made with us in Jesus Christ. The church promises to nurture and love us as we grow in faith. When we are baptized, we receive a sign that we are forever surrounded and protected by God's love.

Holy Communion

The sacrament of Holy Communion is the covenant family meal. By taking Communion, we participate in an ancient act that physically connects us to God and to the larger Christian family; we carry on a family tradition that has brought together Christians for centuries and that Christians will continue for centuries to come.

The Sacraments and Our Faith Walk

Theologian James F. White has said, "One does not understand a mystery, one experiences it."[1] Through baptism and Communion, a community is bound together by God's forgiveness and a vision of the kingdom of God where equality, unity, and justice will reign with love. Coming together on Sunday mornings to baptize or break bread together is not to gain personal access to salvation or to recharge our individual spiritual batteries. This time together is to remember that we are God's children called to spread the gospel and seek peace in our world.

The sacraments are also one of the few times in our lives when we receive without having to give something in return. The sacraments are not about what we have done but about what God can and is doing for us. God has claimed us as God's own in baptism, pouring out the Holy Spirit that will continue to call us, meet us, and empower us as we receive Holy Communion.

SOUL TENDING

- Read your congregation or denomination's ritual of baptism then reflect on the following questions:

    † How have you lived out the promises you have made during each baptism service you have participated in?

    † If you have been baptized, how have your parents and congregation lived up to the promises they made at your baptism?

    † If you were baptized as a teen or an adult, how have you lived out the promises you made at your baptism?

    † How would your church and the world look different if all of these promises were always faithfully kept?

- During a Communion service, pay special attention to the taste, smell, and texture of the bread and wine. Look for God's presence in this moment. Write about your impressions.

Common Worship

Why Worship?

Worship is the gathering of God's people to praise, honor, and glorify God. Common worship is vital to our life of faith. First of all, common worship reminds us that we aren't lone rangers in a wild spiritual frontier. We cannot be Christians in isolation, for it is only together that we are the body of Christ. We sometimes find worship uncomfortable because we end up surrounded not only by the friends we love but also by people we consider hypocrites, by people who irritate us, by those who don't approve of what we are wearing, by toddlers who are noisy and disruptive, and by others whom we just plain don't like. And this motley crew is the very body of Christ with whom we are called to worship and serve. If we worship only with people our own age or only with people we really like, we miss out on the amazing grace of a God who brings us together as a diverse community of forgiven sinners. Worship teaches us that we are made for communion not only with God but also with one another.

We gather in worship to remember who we are and whose we are. In worship, we hear the stories of our family of faith—stories of God's love and God's people that have been passed down through the ages. This "proclamation" part of worship is like listening to grandma tell stories about when dad was young. In listening, we find out more about who we are. We hear the stories of God's grace, and we give thanks for the love of God that will never let us go. In worship, we are nurtured as a family of faith through the sacraments. These visible signs of God's grace claim us as children of God and strengthen us for Christ's service. In her book, *Amazing Grace*, poet and best-selling author Kathleen Norris describes worship as a response to grace and a celebration for God's continued faith in us—God's children.

The Theatre of Worship

Søren Kierkegaard, a nineteenth-century Danish Christian philosopher, explained public worship with the metaphor of the "theatre of worship." In this theatre there are three primary actors—God, the minister, and the congregation. Kierkegaard believed that many of us think of the ministers as the actors in the play and the congregation as the audience. The truth is that the congregation members are the actors with the ministers coaching them to do their best for the audience: God. So, when we leave worship, the question to ask isn't "How was it?" but "How did we do?"

Imagine your church service on any given Sunday. Does the congregation see itself as the actor in the play of worship or as the audience? Is the minister performing for the congregation or coaching the congregation in its performance for God? When you enter the sanctuary on Sunday, will you sit as a passive recipient of worship or be an active participant in the praise and worship offered through word, music and sacraments?

Boring!

Let's face it. Worship doesn't always move us. Worship, especially traditional Sunday morning worship, can be boring and frustrating. We know God is with us when we gather for worship, but sometimes it feels like God is yawning too. In many churches, worship is designed for and by adults— particularly older generations of adults— with little thought given to how the service might be relevant for younger members of the body of Christ. Other congregations try so hard to reach out to young Christians and seekers that they alienate the more seasoned members of the church.

What all Christians, young and old, need to remember is that worship isn't about us. We would all like to participate in worship services that speak to us emotionally and theologically, engage our senses, and include music that we enjoy and appreciate. But we shouldn't get so wrapped up in what we want or expect out of worship that we forgot whom we are worshiping. Our worship, in whatever form it comes should be directed toward God. The challenge is to faithfully approach any worship experience with an attitude of praise and thanksgiving, rather than one of duty and obligation.

Hold on to Your Seats

We gather in worship to praise God, but God also uses worship to transform us. Through the music, the preaching, the prayers, and especially through the sacraments, God is powerfully at work in our lives. The Holy Spirit sometimes grabs hold of us in worship and "moves" us to a new place. In these moments all the actors are playing their parts and we do not have to force the worship experience. The Holy Spirit moves among the faithful offering themselves to God in praise and thanksgiving.

Preparing Our Hearts

Another way we can faithfully engage in worship that we find boring is by preparing our own hearts. We can prepare for worship through prayer. We can pray for the worship leaders; we can pray that God will meet us in worship and speak a personal word to us; we can pray for our hearts to be open to the movement of the Holy Spirit.

We can prepare for worship by spending time with the Scripture text. If a pastor preaches from the lectionary, we can know in advance what the texts will be spend time reflecting on them or even discussing them with others.

We can prepare for worship as we engage in other spiritual disciplines. As we weave Scripture reading, prayer, acts of hospitality, and bearing witness into our daily lives, we will find our minds and hearts open to receive God's grace. As we prepare, we can be confident that God will be with us in common worship and that we will be made one with the body of Christ, the church.

SOUL TENDING

- Get involved: Add your voice to those of the adults who discuss and plan worship in your congregation. Discuss the following questions:

  † What is the most important part of the worship service for older adults in your church? for younger persons? Why?

  † What could our congregation change about worship to attract and engage more people, particularly young people?

  † How might current members of the congregation react to such changes?

- Prepare for worship by praying each day this week for the worship leaders in your congregation and by asking that your own heart would be open to God's leading.

- Talk to your pastor to find out the sermon text for this week's worship service. Prepare for worship by reading and meditating on this Scripture each day.

- Set up a meeting with others interested in worship in your congregation or campus ministry to discuss how you might be more actively engaged in worship.

- Volunteer to read Scripture or lead a prayer in a worship service at your church.

Catechesis and Confirmation

Through baptism, we become part of the family of God. Through confirmation or catechism, we respond publicly to the promise of baptism, pledging to obey and follow Christ. In confirmation, we say what we believe, telling the church and the world that we profess Jesus Christ as Lord and Savior. Confirmation is like beginning a journey. It is a first step in claiming our identity in Christ.

What Is Confirmation?

To be confirmed, you participate in a confirmation class or catechesis depending on your denomination or congregation. Confirmation class and catechesis are two ways of learning the history of our faith—the story of God's people since creation, the story of the Christian church, the story of our denominational traditions, and the story of our congregation. Confirmation class is also an in-depth exploration of the church's doctrine, rituals, and social principles. Catechism teaches the same information through memorization of questions and responses. Both lead up to a confirmation service in which one confirms one's faith in God by proclaiming a statement of belief such as the Apostle's Creed.

By being confirmed, one adopts a mission statement of the church: a creed. A confirmand stands before the congregation and says the Apostles' Creed, the Nicene Creed, or another statement of faith together with the congregation. On its surface, this act may not seem to be a big deal—just reciting some old words that a lot of people don't understand or a rehashing a nice church tradition. But a confirmation or catechism ritual is a very big deal. When one accepts the promises that God has made to her, she claims God's promises. One claims the truth that he belongs to a God who loves him enough to die for him. Confirmation and catechism signify that God has given a person a new identity and the strength and courage to live out that identity. God has called us to live not as lone rangers, but in community—to live and work and laugh and serve with others. When a Christian accepts these promises and responds to them by standing before the church and the world and reciting a creed—and claiming that creed as his or her mission statement—that person's life will never be the same.

Know What You Are Getting Into

As a person prepares to be confirmed, he or she has a special responsibility to learn the basics of the Christian faith. The point is not to memorize a bunch of information and pass a test. Rather, catechetical instruction is intended to help a Christian realize what is at stake in standing before the church and confessing his or her faith in Jesus Christ as Lord and Savior. This decision is not to be taken lightly, and any person making the decision should be fully informed. Confirming one's faith is a commitment that will change the course of one's life in ways that one cannot now imagine. Studying the amazing story of faith and the traditions of the church is an opportunity to learn about the big picture of Christian faith and to ask the tough questions about what it means to be a Christian.

A Language of Faith

As one is confirmed and grows in Christian faith, one learns a new language. Committing to a new worldview involves learning new terminology. Someone who wants to learn to play the oboe must learn to read music. A person who doesn't know what a foul is probably won't excel in basketball. And anyone who decides to pick up and move to Paris should probably learn to speak French.

The same is true for being confirmed as a Christian. Our faith gives us words and phrases that describe who we are and what we believe and that help us talk about the wonder of God. We speak of "redemption" and "grace" and "good news" in ways that might not make sense in a different context. The Christian vocabulary helps us experience and live out our faith. Catechism and confirmation help us learn that new language.

Studying and Learning as a Spiritual Discipline

Catechisms and confirmation classes aren't just for education. Learning about, reflecting on, and discussing the truths of our faith deepen our experience of God and provide a bedrock of trust in difficult times. As we go through life, we will find several opportunities to live out the lessons learned preparing for confirmation.

Read the Apostle's Creed (on page 109)—an ancient statement of faith commonly used in confirmation rituals—pausing on those words and phrases that are especially meaninful to you.

SOUL TENDING

- Reflect and write in response to these questions:

  † If you have been confirmed, what do you remember about the confirmation ceremony? Did you understand what you were doing? How has your confirmation affected the way you have lived since then?

  † What did you learn about God through catechesis or confirmation class that has become real to you since then?

  † If you have not yet been confirmed in the church, what has kept you from making that declaration of faith?

  † What is the importance of catechesis and confirmation in one's life of faith?

- If you haven't yet been confirmed, schedule a time to talk with your pastor or campus minister about what is involved and what steps you need to take to be confirmed.

- If you have been confirmed, keep a journal this week about ways that your profession of faith in Christ makes a difference in your life.

- If your denomination has a formal catechism, choose a question from the catechism to meditate on for the week. Read this question each night before you go to bed and when you wake up in the morning. Look for connections between the question and the answer you chose and the world around you. Write about these connections.

- What is a question you have about faith? Write your own catechism question and answer.

- Memorize the Apostles' Creed (on page 109) or another statement of faith and say it every morning when you wake up as a declaration before you go about your day.

The Apostles' Creed, Ecumenical Version

I believe in God, the Father Almighty,
    creator of heaven and earth.

I believe in Jesus Christ, his only Son, our
    Lord,
  who was conceived by the Holy Spirit,
  born of the Virgin Mary,
  suffered under Pontius Pilate,
  was crucified, died, and was buried;
  he descended to the dead.
  On the third day he rose again;
  he ascended into heaven,
  is seated at the right hand of the Father,
  and will come again to judge the living
    and the dead.

I believe in the Holy Spirit,
  the holy catholic church,
  the communion of saints,
  the forgiveness of sins,
  the resurrection of the body
  and the life everlasting. Amen.

Christian Fellowship

Connected Through Christ

Whenever Christians gather, they do so in the name of Jesus. He is the unseen guest at every congregational meeting, potluck dinner, church softball game, or youth lock-in. Gatherings of Christians are drawn together by the love of Christ and as such are unlike any other get-together. In his letter to the Ephesians Paul reminds us that "unity of the Spirit in the bond of peace" is our goal (Ephesians 4:3). 1 John describes the radical love that causes Christians to regard one another as brothers and sisters. This radical love of neighbor causes people to do things that contradict conventional wisdom, like surrendering all of one's possessions so that they may be used for the good of all people (Acts 2:43-47). While many groups and clubs foster loving communities, do good things, and help people, the church is different precisely because Christ draws us together and motivates our fellowship.

Woven Together as One

It would be a wonderful if we could see the lines that hold our congregations together and hold together the varied relationships that support us within our Christian family. Imagine a string running through your congregation starting with you. Imagine that string running back to someone who has listened to or cared for you. From him or her, to whom might the string extend? If you were to continue this pattern, this one string may link your entire congregation, forming a web criss-crossing your entire

church family, connecting, supporting, and pulling every person closer to one another and to God. Colossians 3:14 says, "Love is more important than anything else. It is what ties everything completely together" (CEV). Our prayer should be that these words are truly represented in each Christian gathering.

Growing Together as One

Every church congregation, fellowship group, or Christian youth organization has its own personality, but there are certain things they hold in common. Read Colossians 3:12-17 (on the right) as if it were a mission statement for your group.

Each congregation or group of Christians will excel at some of the qualities listed in Colossians 3 and have room for growth in others. And each person who belongs to such a congregation or group brings unique gifts that help the others grow in faith and that bring the collective together in Christian fellowship.

> As God's chosen ones, holy and beloved, clothe yourselves with compassion, kindness, humility, meekness, and patience. Bear with one another and, if anyone has a complaint against another, forgive each other; just as the Lord has forgiven you, so you also must forgive. Above all, clothe yourselves with love, which binds everything together in perfect harmony. And let the peace of Christ rule in your hearts, to which indeed you were called in the one body. And be thankful. Let the word of Christ dwell in you richly; teach and admonish one another in all wisdom; and with gratitude in your hearts sing psalms, hymns, and spiritual songs to God. And whatever you do, in word or deed, do everything in the name of the Lord Jesus, giving thanks to God the Father through him.
>
> —Colossians 3:12-17

Why Do We Need One Another?

The image of a fire is often used in describing our need for Christian community: Coals burn longer when they are heaped in a fire with other coals. When one is separated and no longer shares the warmth of the fire, it will cool. If you have had the icy experience of being alone and isolated, then you know how comforting the warmth of true community can be.

Christian fellowship is an important part of our spiritual journey because in it we find persons who have a genuine desire to help us grow and from whom we learn about our faith. We cannot be faithful followers of Jesus Christ in isolation. Even Jesus surrounded himself with others who would be a support system for him—how much more must we need similar support in our journey of faith? A community can bring us joy and rest, hold us accountable to the faith we profess, pray with us in times of need, and join with us in celebrations of praise and thanksgiving.

SOUL TENDING

- Take time each day this week to pray for members of your faith community, individually and collectively.

- Write down the names of those persons who have supported you in your spiritual growth or have made you and important part of their faith journeys. Spend time in prayer each day this week thanking God for your fellowship with these persons.

- Do you think it is significant that the Gospels give us several examples of Jesus eating with friends, relaxing with his disciples, and talking about faith with people who yearn to better know God? How would the New Testament story be different if Jesus had put himself above the community or had lived in isolation?

- How do you participate in Christian fellowship? What other opportunities for fellowship are available to you?

Covenanting

We make commitments every day—unavoidable commitments of work, class, internships, and homework and volunteering to help out around the house, attend meetings of church groups and student organizations, or practice after classes. The commitments we make affect several people to whom we have promised our time, effort, gifts, and service. Some commitments reflect our passions and talents, while we regret making other commitments because of the strain on our time and energy. Whether we honor or break our commitments or agreements is a reflection on our integrity and trustworthiness.

The word that the Bible uses to describe commitments with God is covenant. The scriptural meaning of covenant is to make a lasting agreement with God. Covenants are different from our everyday commitments, promises, and contracts in three ways:

1. **Covenants are always grounded in a relationship with God.**

2. **God never breaks covenants.**

3. **Covenants are always permanent. They cannot be adjusted or amended, only broken.**

Scripture tells the story of God's faithfulness in covenanting with us and, by contrast, of our self-centeredness and idolatry. God remains faithful to the covenants made with Noah and "all flesh that is on the earth" (Genesis 9:1-17) and with Abraham, promising a multitude of descendants and land (Genesis 12:1-9), and renewed through Moses (Deuteronomy 5:1-21). Throughout the history of the Hebrew people, God remained faithful to God's covenant to be their God and not abandon them.

Even though imperfect and disobedient people continually broke their covenants to

God, God eventually offered a lasting and saving covenant through Jesus Christ. Obedience has always been the condition of covenant relationships with God, and Christ's obedience—to the point of dying on a cross—allows us to live eternally in covenant with God. Our faith-history teaches us that through baptism we are adopted into God's family and brought into covenant with God through Jesus Christ. God's incredible love for us, demonstrated through Jesus, saves us from sin and gives us peace.

God is at the center of any covenant. We give up our selfish desires in covenants for the betterment of the relationship and lay ourselves at God's feet for service. We can also make covenants among ourselves in which we ask God to be the glue that holds the covenant group together. Many churches invite members to come together in small groups bound by a covenant. Covenants also are made in a marriage when God is the bond between two people.

SOUL TENDING

- To be faithful to our covenant with God we need the support and accountability of other believers. Read John 15:1-10 on page 115. Write about how the symbol of the vine and the branches helps you better understand the spiritual practice of covenanting.

- Consider the following statements and reflect on or write about your thoughts:

  † I have a difficult time living faithfully to my covenant with God because _____.

  † I can honor my covenant with other Christians by _____.

- Write about a time or experience in the past when you were faithful to God even though you didn't want to be. What effect did this experience have on your relationship with God?

114

- In what area of your life are you struggling to be faithful? Ask a friend to covenant with you to work together on improving that aspect of your life.

- Read the story of Moses in the Book of Exodus. What were the conditions of God's covenant with Moses and with God's people? What enabled Moses to live out the covenant faithfully?

- When have you been unfaithful? Spend time in prayer asking God for forgiveness and thanking God for the grace, love, and encouragement to keep trying.

"I am the true vine, and my Father is the vinegrower. He removes every branch in me that bears no fruit. Every branch that bears fruit he prunes to make it bear more fruit. You have already been cleansed by the word that I have spoken to you. Abide in me as I abide in you. Just as the branch cannot bear fruit by itself unless it abides in the vine, neither can you unless you abide in me. I am the vine, you are the branches. Those who abide in me and I in them bear much fruit, because apart from me you can do nothing. Whoever does not abide in me is thrown away like a branch and withers; such branches are gathered, thrown into the fire, and burned. If you abide in me, and my words abide in you, ask for whatever you wish, and it will be done for you. My Father is glorified by this, that you bear much fruit and become my disciples. As the Father has loved me, so I have loved you; abide in my love. If you keep my commandments, you will abide in my love, just as I have kept my Father's commandments and abide in his love."

—John 15:1-10

115

Community Discernment

Rules or Discernment

Decision-making is a part of daily life. Cereal or toast for breakfast? walk to school or catch a ride? finish the chemistry assignment today or wait until tomorrow? Not only do individuals have to work through large and small decisions, but groups are often called upon to make decisions together.

Most groups use the parliamentary system with Robert's Rules of Order as the final say. Robert's Rules is a classic procedural guide for groups that gather to deliberate and make decision for those whom they represent. The procedures outlined in Robert's Rules lead a group toward making a firm decision. Unfortunately, as helpful as this method can be, it can lead to decisions that alienate a minority of people in the group and disrupt group unity. Winners and losers are always a part of any vote that is not unanimous.

Seeing the Prism of Truth

More and more church groups are using a process of discernment to make decisions in a way that maintains Christian unity. Members of the decision-making body and the larger group that will be affected by the decision spend time together in prayer asking for wisdom and guidance as they consider the decision before them. An attitude that says, "If I can just out-talk people who hold different views, my side will win," has no place in community discernment.

Instead, discerning groups give members an opportunity to consider a topic of discussion from a variety of perspectives.

As different people pray, reflect, express their opinions, and listen carefully to the views of others, the group comes to see the issue in a new way—in a way that more clearly reflects God's will. Because all people are flawed, mistakes will still be made and few decisions will please everyone involved. Still an intentional process of Christian discernment assures all parties that decisions will not be made in haste and that the group is making every effort to be faithful to what God is calling it to do.

The Quadri-what?

Some decisions take all the resources we can muster. We may need to do extensive research and talk with several people before we have enough information to choose action A or action B. The Wesleyan tradition encourages the use of four sources as background for all our decision-making: Scripture, tradition, experience, and reason. (Scholars of John Wesley, the founder of Methodism, have found that Wesley often used these four tools when making decisions. It is important to note that, for Wesley, Scripture was the most important of these tools.)

> I am no longer my own, but thine. Put me to what thouh wilt, rank me with whom thou wilt. Put me to doing, put me to suffering. Let me be employed by thee or laid aside for thee, exalted for thee or brought low by thee. Let me be full, let me be empty. Let me have all things, let me have nothing. I freely and heartily yield all things to thy pleasure and disposal. And now, O glorious and blessed God, Father, Son, and Holy Spirit, thou art mine, and I am thine. So be it. And the covenant which I have made on earth, let it be ratified in heaven. Amen.
>
> —A Covenant Prayer in the Wesleyan Tradition

117

To apply the Wesleyan Quadrilateral to a particular subject, we look first to the Bible and what it says about that topic. Then we consider the instruction of our spiritual ancestors: How has the church historically dealt with similar questions or situations? We apply what we have learned from our own experience and the experiences of others, then employ reason to make the final decision.

For Christians, the ultimate goal when making any decision is to move further along the path toward holiness and life. Some people feel that conventional parliamentary procedures (such as Robert's Rules) move decisions forward more cleanly and quickly. But others suggest that prayerful discernment is invaluable, regardless of how long it takes.

SOUL TENDING

• What big decisions are you facing? How do these decisions affect or involve other people? How can you involve other people in the decision-making process?

• Consider how you might be helpful to others who are wrestling with tough decisions. Pray for them each day this week, asking God to grant them wisdom and guidance.

• Write about a time when you were involved in group discernment or a time when group discernment would have helped a group you were involved with make a better decision.

• Research Quaker John Woolman and how the Society of Friends, through discernment and consensus, was able to voluntarily free their slaves more than one hundred years before the Civil War.

• Attend a meeting of one of the decision-making bodies at your church to see how they work through decisions.

• Read 1 Kings 3:5-14, 16-28 each day this week. What, would you say, was King Solomon's attitude toward decision-making? What was God's response to Solomon?

Acts of Justice and Reconciliation

Society's Understanding of Justice

The family of a murder victim demands justice. The man accused of the crime demands justice from the court system, protecting his rights and guaranteeing him a fair trial. Pro-death penalty groups demand "sure and swift" justice for the accused.

Anti-death penalty groups assert that the man accused of the crime cannot receive justice because he is poor, and that the death penalty is an unjust punishment. The jury hearing the case is told that it is their responsibility to see that justice is served by fairly and impartially applying the law to the facts presented. Later appeals allege justice was denied in the case because the prosecutor acted unfairly, the defense counsel was incompetent, and the judge was biased. These are just a few of the ways the term justice is used everyday.

The everyday understandings of justice are little help in understanding what constitutes "acts of justice" by the church. In order to determine what "acts of justice" are, we must examine the meaning of justice in Scripture.

Justice for the Powerless

Scripture first mentions justice in connection with God's purposes for Abraham, including being a blessing for all nations. "I have chosen [Abraham], that he may charge his children and his household after him to keep the way of the LORD by doing righteousness and justice"

119

(Genesis 18:19a). The justice to be practiced by Abraham will be an example for the world.

Under the laws of Leviticus and Deuteronomy, justice is equated with giving honest testimony in legal proceedings, not showing partiality to either the poor or the rich (Leviticus 19:15; Deuteronomy 16:19). Also appearing for the first time in Deuteronomy is a theme that will define the concept of justice for later generations of Jews and Christians. Those in power have a duty to dispense justice, defined as fair treatment, compassion, and mercy for the weak and those with no power base. Thus, Deuteronomy admonishes the people to protect the rights of aliens, widows, and orphans (Deuteronomy 24:17; 27:19).

Scripture reminds us that, when we forget these priorities, God hears and answers the cries of those we oppress (see Exodus 2:23-25; 22:27; and Psalm 34:17). The prophets also equated justice with fair treatment of the powerless. Amos condemns those who trample the needy and calls them instead to "let justice roll down like waters, and righteousness like an ever-flowing stream" (Amos 5:24). Micah condemns the rulers who have perverted justice and equality (Micah 3:9-12). Micah 6:8 then sums up the desire of God in three instructions, "to do justice, and to love kindness, and to walk humbly with your God."

Christ came to establish God's justice. Scriptures that foretell the coming of Christ speak of the establishment of God's justice. "Here is my servant, whom I uphold, my chosen, in whom my soul delights; I have put my spirit upon him; he will bring forth justice to the nations" (Isaiah 42:1). The coming servant's justice will be a light to all the peoples (Isaiah 51:4). "In those days and at that time I will cause a righteous Branch to spring up for David; and he shall execute justice and righteousness in the land"

(Jeremiah 33:15; see also Matthew 12:18). Christians understand justice to mean that those members of society who are poor, sick, injured, incompetent, defenseless, and living on the margins will not be victimized and will be treated fairly and compassionately. Christians understand that God cares about justice, and that God hears the cries of the oppressed. When we deny justice, we deny God.

SOUL TENDING

• Identify those in your community who are powerless or particularly susceptible, for whatever reason, to being oppressed. Be as specific as possible, even identifying neighborhoods where such persons might live or might be found. Are you a member of any of these groups? Do you participate in the oppression of any of these persons?

• Watch several different news programs daily, praying for God's justice. Identify current events that involve issues of justice and any groups that appear to be victimized, including:

  † issues of taxation

  † criminal legislation

  † embargoes against other nations

  † news and legislation regarding aliens, the homeless, or the mentally incompetent

• Find out how you could join your church's local, regional, or national ministry engaging in justice concerns.

• Read the Book of Amos. List those acts that Amos might condemn if he walked through our cities today. Pray about these issues. What is God calling you to do about these situations?

• If your state uses capital punishment, contact your local bar associations to find out what funds are available to pay for attorneys and investigators for the defense of capital cases and for their prosecution. Pray that the attorneys would seek God's justice in each case.

• Pray daily that God will show you injustice in the world and help you discern what the church can do to address these concerns.

Confession and Forgiveness in Community

We're All in the Same Boat

Some of us may have too low an opinion of ourselves; others of us think too highly of ourselves. In reality every human being has moments when he or she violates a relationship with God or other persons. No person is "better" or "worse" than anyone else; we all need forgiveness. And while Christian disciples need a community of fellow believers to hold us accountable and challenge us to live faithfully, none of us are in a position to pass judgment on a brother or sister (see Matthew 7:1-5). We learn from the story of the woman caught in adultery (John 8:3-11) how Jesus desires for us to live in community. Jesus, the only one without sin who could have condemned the adulterous woman, instead says to the crowd that has gathered to stone her, "Let anyone among you who is without sin be the first to throw a stone at her" (verse 7). Then he tells the woman, "Go your way, and from now on do not sin again" (verse 11).

When we give and receive forgiveness, we also give and receive the gift of transformation. Popular Christian author Donald Miller in *Blue Like Jazz* tells the of a confessional booth set up at a particular university that he describes as "the college where students are most likely to ignore God." In the confessional booth he and his friends did not receive others' confessions but made their own confessions. In one instance Donald confessed to doing too little to

feed the hungry, for not loving those who had persecuted him, and for mixing his spirituality and politics. His confessions, and the confessions of his friends, sparked an interest in Jesus among young people who had written off Christianity. And the confession and forgiveness of others created a new and stronger connection to God that propelled Donald and his friends into action on behalf of those in need.

You Got That?

Jesus spoke frequently about forgiveness. Even after he was crucified, died, and had spent three days in a tomb, Jesus came back to his disciples with the same important message: "Receive the Holy Spirit. If you forgive the sins of any, they are forgiven them" (John 20:22b-23a). Jesus reminded his disciples—those who had betrayed him, those who had fled, and those who were still hiding—of the value of forgiveness. Jesus' forgiveness enables his disciples, then and now, to leave our mistakes and failures behind to go on and do greater things for God. And if we can be forgiven, how much more should we forgive others?

> Jesus said to them again, "Peace be with you. As the Father has sent me, so I send you." When he had said this, he breathed on them and said to them, "Receive the Holy Spirit. If you forgive the sins of any, they are forgiven them; if you retain the sins of any, they are retained."
>
> —John 20:21-23

SOUL TENDING

- Read Colossians 3:12-17 as a standard of Christian behavior. Write about how you have failed to live up to this standard and how could you better exemplify this description of Christian living.

- Memorize Psalm 103:11-12: "For as the heavens are high above the earth, so great is his steadfast love toward those who fear him; as far as the east is from the west, so far he removes our transgressions from us."

- Write a prayer of confession and share it with your pastor or campus minister this week; see if he or she would be willing to let you lead the prayer in worship or as part of a group devotional.

- In worship, pay special attention as the prayer of confession is read. Did you have a new experience praying it this week? Write down your thoughts.

Healing Prayers and Hands

Have you ever witnessed a miraculous healing? ever said a prayer for the health and well-being of a sick friend? ever kissed a toddler's sore finger or kept a bedside vigil with loved ones? How have you experienced the power of healing prayers and hands in your life?

As believers, we ask God for healing mercies. We gather to pray, to anoint, and to lay hands on those in pain. Our prayers reassure and point to the presence of God with us. Our touch reminds the patient of the healing touch of Jesus. (See, for example, Mark 5:25-34 and John 9:1-12.)

God couples the prayers and compassionate gestures of believers with other gifted hands, heads, and hearts to bring about health and well-being. It is God who "kisses and makes it better."

Do You Believe?

The disciples' efforts to heal a boy possessed by a demon had failed (Mark 9:14-29). Doubt and skepticism seemed reasonable for all involved. But the boy's father was desperate. He pleaded with Jesus, saying, "If you are able to do anything, have pity on us and help us" (verse 22). Jesus was incredulous and replied, "If you are able!—All things can be done for the one

> Jesus said to him, "If you are able!—All things can be done for the one who believes." Immediately the father of the child cried out, "I believe, help my unbelief!"
>
> —Mark 9:23-24

125

who believes." Jesus questions the father's belief. Picture the father kneeling on the group with his hands folded with his fingers intertwined. He answers as if one hand believes while the other hand doubts. In moments of desperation and crisis many of us badly want Jesus' help and healing but cannot quite believe that we could receive such grace. In those situations we must put our confidence in Christ and pray as the father in this Scripture does, "I believe; help my unbelief!" (verse 24).

Prayers and Presence

The presence of believers with the sick and distressed makes room for the light of Christ. This light reveals the pain, gives ear to the sighs, and steps in to make all things possible.

Healing prayers, anointing, and laying on of hands are acts of compassion and mercy. The spiritual practice of healing is a ministry of presence. We listen carefully to those in pain. We pray for God's healing. We touch and bear the healing light of Christ.

The importance of this presence is seen most clearly in the story of Jesus' healing a paralytic, Luke 5:17-26. The paralytic's friends were not only sympathetic. They did not just call or send an e-mail. These four heroes carried their friend, dug a hole in a roof and lowered him directly in front of Jesus. Healing is more than medicine; it is the presence and faith of a community of believers who will believe when the sick cannot and who will put their faith into action.

Does God Say, "No"?

Sometimes, because we pray for healing, we expect that God will heal our loved ones, either physically or spiritually. Then when what we expected doesn't happen, we blame God for not answering our prayers. But often God's

126

plan and God's timing are different than we think they should be. We can continue to pray and look for God's healing in unexpected ways.

SOUL TENDING

- In communities of faith, God uses the hearts and hands of the church to reach out with healing. Make a list of persons in your community who need physical or spiritual healing. Take time now to pray for them by name.

- Intercessory prayer—praying into the lives of others—is healing prayer. Many communities of faith have a prayer chain that operates around the clock. Phone calls and e-mails connect those who pray for the health and well-being of others. Volunteer to be part of a prayer chain or get online and create a prayer circle of your own.

- Practice the spiritual discipline of healing in community. Gather believers for a time of healing prayers, anointing, and the laying on of hands.

- Put your healing hands to work in practical and compassionate ways. Check with your area hospital or hospice house. Many are in need of volunteers who would offer time and a healing touch. You might rock a baby, rub tired feet, or stroke a cramped hand. Pray as you do and invite others to pray their way into the lives of those you touch.

- Start a prayer journal. Keep track of persons as you pray for them. Pay attention to what God does with the prayers of believers and with the gifted hands, heads, and hearts of doctors and other trained health specialists. Witness to the healing light of Christ. Give thanks and praise in the company of other believers.

- If you are gifted and called to do so, be trained as a Stephen Minister—a layperson trained to give one-on-one care to members of his or her congregation. Check *www.stepheministry.org* for more information.

- Contact The Upper Room Prayer Center to see how you can become involved in this healing ministry. Visit them at *www.upperroom.org.*

Loving Hospitality

What's the first thing that pops into your head when you think of hospitality? Do you think of elegant parties? frantic preparations? five-star restaurants? the pleasant warmth of a hotel jacuzzi?

The spiritual practice of loving hospitality is about accepting desperate phone calls in the middle of the night. It's about welcoming the lost and making room for travelers. It's about belonging and having a place at the table. Hospitality is the warmth of love given and received.

Host and Guest

The Greek word *xenos* means both "host" and "guest." The root word of hospitality—*hospes*—claims both the host and guest as one. Martha received Jesus as a guest (Luke 10:38-42). After he had received Martha's gift of hospitality, he became the host and offered his own gifts to Martha's sister Mary. The men along the road to Emmaus (Luke 24:13-35) offered to host and feed a "stranger" who just happened to be the risen Christ. Jesus, in turn, became a host to these hospitable men by breaking the bread over dinner. Still today, we have opportunities to welcome and host the risen Christ. Jesus tell us that whenever we welcome, visit, feed, and clothe the "least of these," we welcome, visit, feed, and clothe Jesus himself (Matthew 25:40).

Making Room

From beginning to end, Scripture calls us to love our neighbor. The Old Testament law directs God's children to love the stranger, open our hearts and hands to the poor and needy, and eat with our enemies. The Gospels summon believers to welcome and give care to all people, especially those who are most in need. The call to hospitality is clear. The question is how to live out this call.

After the tumultuous events of Christ's crucifixion and resurrection, fear forced the disciples to lock the door. Fear kept the disciples a "safe distance" away from danger and closed them off from the outside world. Fear can also keep us from offering hospitality. Welcoming strangers can be risky, even dangerous. Meeting the needs of brothers and sisters who are hungry or homeless requires sacrifice and stepping out of our comfort zone. Reaching out to those whom society deems undesirable or menacing can make us the subject of scorn and ridicule.

But Jesus calls us to overcome our fears and be hospitable to all persons. We are to reach out help those in need and do simple things, such as being a listening ear when someone needs to "spill it." When we open the doors of our hearts to receive God's love, that love smothers us with a genuine concern for all persons. When our hearts are open, our doors are too.

The risen Christ stood among his first disciples (see John 20:19-23) and still stands among us today. He offers to exchange our fears and anxious feelings for peace and comfort. This peace has the power to change *hostis* (enemy) into *hospes* (guest). Is God knocking on the door? Make room to open it!

SOUL TENDING

- Strangers become friends at the Lord's Table. The familiar actions and stories make room for us to accept and receive. We welcome one another and Christ into our lives as the bread and cup are lifted and shared. Seek an opportunity to share the sacrament of Holy Communion as a guest of another congregation.

- At one time or another, we are all strangers. Pray the Scripture from Deuteronomy below. Invite God to give you a stranger's insight into loving hospitality. Listen for ways you might reach out to someone as one stranger to another.

- Form a hospitality team within your congregation or campus fellowship. Volunteer to take food to shut-ins, to welcome visitors to the community, or perform other acts of hospitality.

> You shall also love the stranger, for you were strangers in the land of Egypt.
>
> —Deuteronomy 10:19

Ordination

Have you ever felt called to ministry? Perhaps someone has asked you that question. Maybe you've asked yourself. The idea may seem strange or unappealing or even frightening: Me—*ordained to be a minister?*

All Are Called

Christians believe that all disciples of Jesus are called to some form of ministry. When we are baptized and when we claim our baptism through confirmation or a profession of faith, we are responding to this call to ministry. Scripture tells us that God has given each of us different spiritual gifts (1 Corinthians 12) in order to build up the body of Christ (Ephesians 4:1-16). Some minister as schoolteachers, as nurses and physicians, as business executives, or as computer technicians and mechanics.

> I had pursued several other paths in college, and none seemed to lead me anywhere. One summer, while working on a camp staff, I had the sense that I should serve full-time in Christian ministry. And when I said yes to this leading, I felt an inner peace.
>
> —Ken Carter, an ordained elder in The United Methodist Church

We also believe that God calls some to ordained ministry. The call may not come in the form of an audible voice but might instead be a silent nudge or a persistent thought. For some the call is clear and obvious, but others spend years wrestling with God's call to ordained ministry.

Some Are Set Apart

Ordained ministry begins with a call from God, sometimes identified as an "inner call." This inner call is usually "echoed" in an outer call. Faithful friends, family members, teachers, and leaders are good people to talk with about God's call in our lives, whether it's a call to ordained ministry or a call to minister through some other profession. The church—our congregation, our denomination, and the church as a whole—can also affirm our call. In this way the call of God may become audible, as God speaks to the individual through the church. When a person is ordained, he or she is "set apart" for specific service to God.

In most cases, young women and men exploring ordination are given mentors who help them discern and pray about this direction for their lives. They are not in this journey alone. The call to ordained ministry is also a call to prepare. College and seminary programs in Scripture, ministry, ethics, and theology build a solid foundation, and internships give candidates practical experience.

The Power Belongs to God

Candidates for ordination also develop relationships with persons who are currently ordained. Candidates learn first hand that clergy are human, with faults, failures, and sin but also with commitments to seek God's will in the work they do.

One of the heresies of the early church was that a priest had to be perfect for the Communion service to be valid. By contrast, the Bible says that all of us, including those who are ordained ministers, have the treasure of the gospel of Jesus Christ in "clay jars, so that it may be made clear that this extraordinary power belongs to God and does not come from us" (2 Corinthians 4:7).

God uses ordinary men and women in the work of ordained ministry. Some are effective speakers, while others are not. Some are great listeners, while others are not. Some are evangelists, missionaries, teachers, and organizers—all of these gifts are important and can be of service to God and the world.

All Christians are called to some form of ministry. Some are "set apart" for ordained ministry. What is God saying to you? How will you respond?

SOUL TENDING

- Schedule a conversation with an ordained minister about his or her work. What is satisfying about the job? What is most challenging? What sustains him or her? What is most important to him or her about the work of a minister?

- Have a conversation with an adult whose judgment and wisdom have helped you in the past. Ask him or her to pray with you and to listen as you consider different paths of ministry.

- Ask to "shadow" (follow alongside) an ordained minister as he or she works one afternoon. Discuss the experience afterward.

- Memorize Isaiah 6:8, meditating upon the ministry to which God is sending you.

> Then I heard the voice of the Lord saying, "Whom shall I send, and who will go for us?" And I said, "Here am I; send me!"
>
> —Isaiah 6:8

133

Spiritual Friendship

Most of us have friends with whom we enjoy hanging out, but what takes a friendship to a deeper level? Perhaps two people endure trials together or, on the other side, share such great joy that they are bound to each other. Maybe friends are compatible because of common interests and values and develop a level of trust that enables them to share the deep recesses of their hearts. Other friends may have known each other so long that they can finish each other's sentences. Friends are an important and beautiful part of life.

Friends in the Spirit

The Christian church has a long tradition of spiritual friendship as a way to grow closer to God. In any close friendship, two people will share what is most important in their lives: hopes, dreams, fears, and concerns about relationships, as well as details of their everyday lives. In a spiritual friendship two people may also share such things, but they will also intentionally focus on each person's relationship with God.

John Wesley used to ask, "How is it with your soul?" That question is a good starting point for a spiritual friendship. In spiritual friendship people agree to discuss openly their spiritual lives in a way that encourages each person to grow in faith. Spiritual friends might set aside a regular time to talk about what is happening in their prayer lives, how the words of a sermon struck them, or an image that came to mind during a period of silence.

Beginning a Spiritual Friendship

Spiritual friends trust each other and pledge to keep conversations confidential. They practice holy listening, are patient with each other, and celebrate simple joys together. The goal of a spiritual friendship is for each person to come to better know God and to progress along his or her spiritual journey.

> The soul of Jonathan was bound to the soul of David, and Jonathan loved him as his own soul.
>
> —1 Samuel 18:1b

Young people and older adults both need spiritual friends. Persons new to the faith and those who have been practicing Christians for decades both need spiritual friendships in which to discuss their faith, ask difficult questions, wrestle with doubts, and talk about revelations.

Mary and her relative and friend Elizabeth had this type of friendship. When Mary found out she was pregnant she went "with haste" to see Elizabeth. (Luke 1:39-45) When we want to celebrate we seek out our friends. When we are overwhelmed by life we go to our friends. When we are not sure whether certain circumstances are worthy of celebration or fear, we run to our spiritual friends for a listening ear, support, and prayer.

SOUL TENDING

- Think of who might be a possible spiritual friend for you. If no one immediately comes to mind, ask God to help you find a person who can help you grow spiritually (and whom you can help grow spiritually).

- Take time to write about what you might want and need in a spiritual friendship. List any questions you have related to your faith journey or issues you face in your relationship with God.

- Read about David and Jonathan (1 Samuel 18–23, especially 18:1-4; 23:15-18). How was theirs a spiritual friendship? What friendship have you had that helped you better know God? Thank God for your spiritual friends in prayer each day this week.

- Write down what qualities you think are most important in a spiritual friend. Then make an honest appraisal of yourself: In what ways could you be a good spiritual friend to someone else? Are there aspects of yourself that might need to change before you could open yourself to another's intimate journey with God?

- Read and meditate on the story of Mary and Elizabeth (Luke 1:39-45) each day this week. What can you learn from their spiritual friendship?

136

Being the Body of Christ

Sometimes Christians focus so much on personal salvation and a personal relationship with Jesus Christ, that we lose sight of what Paul tells us about being the church: "Now you are the body of Christ and individually members of it" (1 Corinthians 12:27).

About as Human as You Can Get

A source of great frustration yet great comfort for Christians is the reality that the church is about as human and as frail as you can get. All the sins of humanity play out in the church. This is frustrating because Christians, quite understandably and properly, expect the church, the body of Christ, to rise above people's sinful nature. On the other hand, it is a source of comfort because—despite our shortfalls and weaknesses—God has made us the body of Christ and empowers us to be the presence of Christ in the world.

The Letter to the Colossians gives us a sense of what it means to be Christ's body. In it, Paul tells us to clothe ourselves in love, letting the peace of Christ rule in our hearts, treat one another as brothers and sisters, and make everything we do something we do in the name of Jesus Christ (Colossians 3:12-17).

The Greatest of These Is Love

Paul tells the church, "Love!" "Let love be genuine; hate what is evil, hold fast to what is good; love one another with mutual affection" (Romans 12:9-10a). "Owe no one anything, except to love one another" (Romans 13:8a). "Knowledge puffs up, but love binds up" (1 Corinthians 8:1b).

137

"Live in love, as Christ loved us" (Ephesians 5:2).
Many other Scriptures speak of loving others. The
point is this: No one—especially God—devotes that
much ink to something that is not important. Love is
the guiding principle of conduct for the body of
Christ.

First Corinthians 13, the so-called "love chapter," is
often read at weddings. However, Paul was not
writing to a newly married couple but to the church at
Corinth and to us, the body of Christ. Imagine a
church that lived by these words:

> Love is patient; love is kind; love is not envious or
> boastful or arrogant or rude. It does not insist on its
> own way; it is not irritable or resentful; it does not
> rejoice in wrongdoing, but rejoices in the truth. It
> bears all things, believes all things, hopes all things,
> endures all things.
>
> Love never ends. (1 Corinthians 13:4-8a)

Brothers and Sisters

At one time it was common for people in the church
to address one another as "brother" and "sister." The
practice still exists in some traditions and has biblical
roots. Paul used these words over one hundred twenty
times to address his churches, the body of Christ. In
contrast, he only used "saints" about forty times.

If we speak and come to think of one another as
brothers and sisters—as family—we are more likely to
act toward one another with love and care. Paul's use
of "brother" and "sister" was quite intentional. Paul
prayed that the church, the body of Christ, would
understand itself as a family with Christ as its head.

Do It in the Name of Christ

The initialism "WWJD?"—What would Jesus do?—was very popular in Christian circles in the 1990s. While WWJD? is certainly a good question to ask ourselves, Paul offers a more challenging and meaningful standard of behavior: "Whatever you do, in word or deed, do everything in the name of the Lord Jesus, giving thanks to God the Father through him" (Colossians 3:17).

Some of the unloving and hateful things we all have done—unkind words spoken in anger, gossip we couldn't resist spreading, or the thoughtless neglect of some simple act of kindness—seem all the more offensive when you remember, "I am doing this in the name of my Lord, Jesus Christ." Understanding yourself as part of the body of Christ means that those words are implied in everything you say and do. When you act out of love, you do so in the name of Christ. When you act out of hate, you do so in the name of Christ. You can't blame the bad acts on an evil twin. The good you do builds and strengthens the body of Christ. The evil you do tears down and weakens the body of Christ.

Bringing It All Together

The body of Christ is a creation of and powered by the Spirit of God. When it operates at its best, it is a family—brothers and sisters—led by Christ, acting in the name of Christ, out of love for one another and love for God's creation.

Years ago, a cartoonist named Rube Goldberg drew cartoons of strange and complex gadgets, machines that filled whole rooms. Windmills or mice on treadmills might have a small role in operating these strange contraptions. They also contained countless wheels and pulleys, gears turning clockwise and counterclockwise. They were always designed to perform an ironically simple task: a room-sized machine that buttered a piece of toast or that turned on a light "automatically," for example. "Rube Goldberg" came to describe a complicated and inefficient, but practical device or organization.

The church is often God's "Rube Goldberg device." Conflicted, inefficient, totally broken down in parts, it operates only because God wills it to. The miracle of Christ's presence is confirmed in the reality that God has preserved the church, in all its brokenness, for nearly than two thousand years; and the church, in all its brokenness, continues to minister to the world in important and vital ways.

The church has unrealized potential that is achievable only through the power of God. When the people of the church come to understand themselves as the body of Christ, the living presence of Christ, acting out of love and in Jesus' name, the world truly sees the presence of Christ.

SOUL TENDING

- Keep a journal listing everything you have done throughout the day. Include conversations you had, disagreements with others, acts of ministry, and anything else that occurred. Understanding that we do everything in the name of Christ, use a colored marker to highlight those things that you believe God could use to strengthen the body of Christ. Using a different color, highlight those that you believed weakened the body of Christ. Pray about both.

- For the next week, watch or listen to several different news programs each day. Read a newspaper daily. Take notes on current events that demonstrate the body of Christ in action. Also look for stories that you believe reflect poorly on the body of Christ. At the end of the week, review all your notes. How visible is the body of Christ in the news media and how is the body of Christ portrayed?

- A great irony of Christian history is the fragmentation of the body of Christ into many different Christian traditions. Using a phone book, identify five different Christian traditions represented in your area. Find websites sponsored by these traditions. Review their statements of belief. Also so some research on your denominations stated beliefs. Pick one or two other traditions and list four or five ways their beliefs differ from those of your tradition and four or five ways they are the same. Try to determine if you could worship together, sharing the sacrament of Holy Communion.

- Pray daily for the body of Christ in all its unity and in all its brokenness.

142

Contributors

Anne Broyles
Stillness and Silence, Discernment, Honoring the Body, Seeking and Granting Forgiveness, Stewardship of Household Economics and Money, Stewardship of Creation and Time, Spiritual Direction, Solitude, Christian Fellowship, Community Discernment, Confession and Forgiveness in Community, Spiritual Friendship

Beverly Burton
Testimony

Ken Carter
Self-Denial, Testimony, Ordination

Rachel Cousart
Self-Denial

Drew Dyson
Introduction

Dennis J. Meaker
Acts of Justice and Reconciliation, Being the Body of Christ

Barbara K. Mittman
Forgiveness, Giving Thanks and Praise, Speaking the Truth in Love, Living Simply, Healing Prayers and Hands, Loving Hospitality

Kara Lassen Oliver
Devotional Reading, Chastity, Bible Study, Sacraments, Covenanting

Robin Pippin
Lectio Divina

Kyle Roberson
Meditation, Fasting, Keeping the Sabbath

Amy Scott Vaughn
Common Worship, Catechesis and Confirmation

Jennifer A. Youngman
Prayer From a Repentent Heart, Singing From the Soul

Kara Lassen Oliver, General Editor

Kara holds a Master of Divinity from Vanderbilt Divinity School and has spent the past decade working with and for youth. She has contributed to several Abingdon Press titles as a writer and editor. She and her husband, Jeff, live in Nashville with their two children, Claire and Carter.

> "You are the light of the world. A city built on a hill cannot be hid. No one after lighting a lamp puts it under the bushel basket, but on the lampstand, and it gives light to all in the house. In the same way, let your light shine before others, so that they may see your good works and give glory to your Father in heaven."
>
> —Matthew 5:14-16

144